First World War

and Army of Occupation

War Diary

France, Belgium and Germany

41 DIVISION
123 Infantry Brigade
Durham Light Infantry
20th Battalion
4 May 1916 - 31 October 1917

WO95/2639/1

The Naval & Military Press Ltd
www.nmarchive.com
Published in association with The National Archives

Published by

The Naval & Military Press Ltd

Unit 10 Ridgewood Industrial Park,

Uckfield, East Sussex,

TN22 5QE England

Tel: +44 (0) 1825 749494

www.naval-military-press.com

www.nmarchive.com

This diary has been reprinted in facsimile from the original. Any imperfections are inevitably reproduced and the quality may fall short of modern type and cartographic standards.

Contents

Document type	Place/Title	Date From	Date To
Heading	WO95/2639/1		
Heading	20th Bn Durham Lt Infy May 1916-1917 Oct		
Heading	20th (Service) Battalion Durham Light Infantry 123rd Infantry Brigade. War Diary.		
War Diary	Aldershot Southampton	04/05/1916	04/05/1916
War Diary	Havre	05/05/1916	06/05/1916
War Diary	Strazeele	07/05/1916	27/05/1916
War Diary	Noote Boom	28/05/1916	28/05/1916
War Diary	Le Bizet	29/05/1916	29/05/1916
War Diary	Le Touquet Station	30/05/1916	31/05/1916
Heading	20th (Service) Battalion Durham Light Infantry. War Diary		
War Diary	In Tranches (Le Bizet Night Subsecton In 91. 92 & 93)	31/05/1916	04/06/1916
War Diary	Armentieres	05/06/1916	10/06/1916
War Diary	Armentieres In Trenches	10/06/1916	10/06/1916
War Diary	In Trenches	11/06/1916	15/06/1916
War Diary	In Trenches Armentieres	16/06/1916	24/06/1916
War Diary	In Trenches Armentieres In Trenches	24/06/1916	30/06/1916
Miscellaneous	With reference to Battalion O.O. No. 9 of the 27th inst.	30/06/1916	30/06/1916
Operation(al) Order(s)	Operation Order No. 9 By Lt. Col. K. J. W Leather, Comdg. 20th Bn Durham Light Infantry	27/06/1916	27/06/1916
Miscellaneous	Headquarters, 20th Bn Durham Light Infantry	02/07/1916	02/07/1916
Miscellaneous	Detail Of Operation "A" With Gas And Smoke.		
Miscellaneous	Headquarters 20th Bn Durham Light Infantry.	01/07/1916	01/07/1916
War Diary	Trenches 91-93 near Le Bizet.	01/07/1916	02/07/1916
War Diary	Armentieres	03/07/1916	06/07/1916
War Diary	Le Bizet	07/07/1916	13/07/1916
War Diary	In Trenches (91-98)	14/07/1916	14/07/1916
War Diary	In Trenches	14/07/1916	25/07/1916
War Diary	Le Bizet	26/07/1916	26/07/1916
War Diary	Armentieres	27/07/1916	30/07/1916
Miscellaneous	123rd Inf. Bde.	04/06/1916	04/06/1916
Miscellaneous	20th (S) Bn. Durham Light Infantry	01/07/1916	01/07/1916
Miscellaneous	20th (S) Bn. Durham Light Infantry	08/07/1916	08/07/1916
Miscellaneous	20th (S) Bn. Durham Light Infantry	15/07/1916	15/07/1916
Miscellaneous	20th (S) Bn. Durham Light Infantry	22/07/1916	22/07/1916
Miscellaneous	20th (S) Bn. Durham Light Infantry	29/07/1916	29/07/1916
Operation(al) Order(s)	20th (S) Bn. Durham Light Infantry Operation Order No. 12	20/07/1916	20/07/1916
Operation(al) Order(s)	Operation Order No. 1 By Major Hills, O.C. Enterprise.	25/07/1916	25/07/1916
Miscellaneous	Appendix Equipment For Personnel.		
Miscellaneous	O.C. 20th Bn Durham Light Infantry	28/07/1916	28/07/1916
Miscellaneous	123rd Infantry Brigade.	28/07/1916	28/07/1916
War Diary	Armentieres	31/07/1916	31/07/1916
War Diary	Armentieres And Trenches 91-95 (Le Bizet Area)	01/08/1916	01/08/1916
War Diary	In Trenches	02/08/1916	12/08/1916
War Diary	In Trenches Armentieres	12/08/1916	13/08/1916
War Diary	Armentieres	14/08/1916	16/08/1916
War Diary	Armentieres and Steenwerck	16/08/1916	16/08/1916
War Diary	Mont Des Cats Area	17/08/1916	22/08/1916

War Diary	Bailleul	23/08/1916	23/08/1916
War Diary	Longpre Yarcourt-Bussus	24/08/1916	24/08/1916
War Diary	Yaucourt-Bussus.	25/08/1916	30/08/1916
Heading	War Diary 20th Durham L. I. From 17th To Sept 30th 1916		
War Diary	Yaucourt Bussus	01/09/1916	06/09/1916
War Diary	Yaucourt Bussus Near Becordel	06/08/1916	06/08/1916
War Diary	Near Becordel	08/09/1916	10/09/1916
War Diary	In Trenches	11/09/1916	13/09/1916
War Diary	Nr. Pommiers Redoubt.	14/09/1916	14/09/1916
War Diary	Check Line Original Front Line.	15/09/1916	15/09/1916
War Diary	Original Front Line.	16/09/1916	16/09/1916
War Diary	Flers Defences	17/09/1916	18/09/1916
War Diary	Near Becordel	19/09/1916	27/09/1916
War Diary	East Of Mametz	28/09/1916	28/09/1916
War Diary	In Trenches.	29/09/1916	30/09/1916
Miscellaneous	20th (Ser) Bn Durham Light Infantry.	08/09/1916	08/09/1916
Heading	War Diary 20th (S) Bn Durham Light Infantry From Oct. 1st 1916 to Oct 31st 1916 Indium		
War Diary	Trenches in Front of Flers	01/10/1916	01/10/1916
War Diary	Pommiers Redoubt	02/10/1916	02/10/1916
War Diary	Mametz Wood	03/10/1916	07/10/1916
War Diary	Switch Trench	08/10/1916	08/10/1916
War Diary	Front Line	09/10/1916	10/10/1916
War Diary	Mametz Wood	11/10/1916	12/10/1916
War Diary	Dernancourt	13/10/1916	17/10/1916
War Diary	Citerne	18/10/1916	19/10/1916
War Diary	Godewaersvelde	20/10/1916	21/10/1916
War Diary	Reninghelst	22/10/1916	23/10/1916
War Diary	Trenches	24/10/1916	29/10/1916
War Diary	Reninghelst	30/10/1916	31/10/1916
Operation(al) Order(s)	123rd Infantry Brigade Order No. 34	30/09/1916	30/09/1916
Miscellaneous	20th (S) Bn. Durham Light Infantry.	07/10/1916	07/10/1916
Miscellaneous	20th (S) Bn. Durham Light Infantry.	14/10/1916	14/10/1916
Miscellaneous	20th (S) Bn. Durham Light Infantry.	21/10/1916	21/10/1916
Operation(al) Order(s)	123rd Infantry Brigade Order No. 38	10/10/1916	10/10/1916
Miscellaneous	XV Corps. A.C.1052/L.5 41st Div. No. A. 4/53	22/10/1916	22/10/1916
Miscellaneous	Fourth Army No. 335 (G.S)	27/10/1916	27/10/1916
Heading	War Diary of 20th (S) Bn Durham Light Infantry. from November 1st 1916 to November 30th 1916		
War Diary	Reninghelst	01/11/1916	02/11/1916
War Diary	Trenches	03/11/1916	09/11/1916
War Diary	Ontario Camp	10/11/1916	15/11/1916
War Diary	Trenches	16/11/1916	22/11/1916
War Diary	Ontario Camp	23/11/1916	27/11/1916
War Diary	Trenches	28/11/1916	30/11/1916
Miscellaneous	20th (S) Bn Durham. L. I. (1) Strength State.	04/11/1916	04/11/1916
Miscellaneous	20th (S) Bn Durham. L. I. (2) Strength State.	11/11/1916	11/11/1916
Miscellaneous	20th (S) Bn Durham. L. I. (3) Strength State.	18/11/1916	18/11/1916
Miscellaneous	20th (S) Bn Durham. L. I. (4) Strength State.	25/11/1916	25/11/1916
War Diary	Trenches	01/12/1916	03/12/1916
War Diary	Ontario Camp	04/12/1916	09/12/1916
War Diary	Trenches	10/12/1916	15/12/1916
War Diary	Ontario Camp	16/12/1916	22/12/1916
War Diary	Trenches	23/12/1916	31/12/1916
War Diary	Trenches Camp	31/12/1916	31/12/1916

War Diary	Ontario Camp	01/01/1917	02/01/1917
War Diary	Trenches	03/01/1917	07/01/1917
War Diary	Ontario Camp	08/01/1917	13/01/1917
War Diary	Trenches	14/01/1917	21/01/1917
War Diary	Ontario Camp	22/01/1917	28/01/1917
War Diary	Trenches	29/01/1917	31/01/1917
Miscellaneous	20th Bn. Durham L. I. Strength State.	13/01/1917	13/01/1917
Miscellaneous	20th Bn. Durham L. I. Strength State.	20/01/1917	20/01/1917
Miscellaneous	20th Bn. Durham L. I. Strength State.	00/01/1917	00/01/1917
Miscellaneous	20th Bn. Durham L. I. Strength State.	06/01/1917	06/01/1917
War Diary	Trenches	01/02/1917	03/02/1917
War Diary	Ontario Camp	04/02/1917	10/02/1917
War Diary	Trenches	10/02/1917	16/02/1917
War Diary	Ontario Camp.	17/02/1917	22/02/1917
War Diary	Trenches	23/02/1917	27/02/1917
War Diary	Ontario Camp	28/02/1917	28/02/1917
Miscellaneous	Account of Patrol on the Night	24/02/1917	24/02/1917
Miscellaneous	20th Durham Light Infantry Strength State.	03/02/1917	03/02/1917
Miscellaneous	20th Durham Light Infantry Strength State.	10/02/1917	10/02/1917
Miscellaneous	20th Durham Light Infantry Strength State.	17/02/1917	17/02/1917
Miscellaneous	20th Durham Light Infantry Strength State.	24/02/1917	24/02/1917
War Diary	Ontario Camp	01/03/1917	04/03/1917
War Diary	Trenches	05/03/1917	11/03/1917
War Diary	Ontario Camp	12/03/1917	17/03/1917
War Diary	In The Trenches	17/03/1917	23/03/1917
War Diary	Ontario Camp	24/03/1917	30/03/1917
War Diary	In The Trenches	31/03/1917	31/03/1917
Miscellaneous	20th (S) Bn. Durham Light Infantry.	03/03/1917	03/03/1917
Miscellaneous	20th (S) Bn. Durham Light Infantry.	10/03/1917	10/03/1917
Miscellaneous	20th (S) Bn. Durham Light Infantry.	17/03/1917	17/03/1917
Miscellaneous	20th (S) Bn. Durham Light Infantry.	24/03/1917	24/03/1917
Miscellaneous	20th (S) Bn. Durham Light Infantry.	31/03/1917	31/03/1917
War Diary	Trenches	01/04/1917	05/04/1917
War Diary	Ontario Camp	06/04/1917	06/04/1917
War Diary	Steenvoorde Area	07/04/1917	07/04/1917
War Diary	Noordpeene Area	08/04/1917	08/04/1917
War Diary	Eperlecques	09/04/1917	23/04/1917
War Diary	Waemers-Cappel	24/04/1917	24/04/1917
War Diary	Steenvoorde Area	25/04/1917	25/04/1917
War Diary	Ontario Camp	26/04/1917	30/04/1917
Map	Appendix III		
Miscellaneous	20th (S) Bn. Durham Light Infantry. Appendix I	05/04/1917	05/04/1917
Miscellaneous	20th (S) Bn. Durham Light Infantry. Appendix II	14/04/1917	14/04/1917
Miscellaneous	Remarks by G. O. C Brigade (Gen Gordon) Practice attack Appendix IV	02/04/1917	02/04/1917
Miscellaneous	20th (S) Bn. Durham Light Infantry. Appendix V	24/04/1917	24/04/1917
Miscellaneous	20th (S) Bn. Durham Light Infantry. Appendix VI	28/04/1917	28/04/1917
Heading	War Diary Of 20th (S) Bn. Durham Light Infantry from 1st May 1917-31st May 1917		
War Diary	Ontario Camp	01/05/1917	02/05/1917
War Diary	Micmac Camp	03/05/1917	11/05/1917
War Diary	Trenches	12/05/1917	19/05/1917
War Diary	Trenches & Micmac Camp	19/05/1917	19/05/1917
War Diary	Micmac Camp	20/05/1917	31/05/1917
Miscellaneous	20th (S) Bn. Durham Light Infantry Daily State.	05/05/1917	05/05/1917
Miscellaneous	20th (S) Bn. Durham L. I. Daily State.	12/05/1917	12/05/1917

Miscellaneous	20th (S) Bn. Durham L. I. Daily State.	19/05/1917	19/05/1917
Miscellaneous	20th (S) Bn. Durham L. I. Daily State.	26/05/1917	26/05/1917
War Diary	Micmac Camp	01/06/1917	01/06/1917
War Diary	Wendote Camp	02/06/1917	05/06/1917
War Diary	Trenches G. 16. O.2 Time	06/06/1917	06/06/1917
War Diary	Near St Eloi.	07/06/1917	12/06/1917
War Diary	R Line (Near Bois Confleant)	12/06/1917	12/06/1917
War Diary	R Line.	13/06/1917	14/06/1917
War Diary	Old. R Line. (Near Bois Confleant)	15/06/1917	15/06/1917
War Diary	Old R. Line.	16/06/1917	21/06/1917
War Diary	O 4 A	22/06/1917	23/06/1917
War Diary	Spoil Bank	24/06/1917	26/06/1917
War Diary	Norfolk Road	27/06/1917	30/06/1917
Miscellaneous	Major Comdg 20th Durham.		
Miscellaneous	Appendix I	07/06/1917	07/06/1917
War Diary	In The Trenches Mubrumbidge Camp.	01/07/1917	01/07/1917
War Diary	Mont Des Cats.	02/07/1917	20/07/1917
War Diary	Kenora Camp Westoutre	21/07/1917	24/07/1917
War Diary	Wood Camp Trenches	25/07/1917	25/07/1917
War Diary	Trenches	26/07/1917	26/07/1917
War Diary	In The Trenches	27/07/1917	31/07/1917
Operation(al) Order(s)	20th Durham Light Infantry Operation Order No. 88 Appendix II	30/05/1917	30/05/1917
Miscellaneous	20th Durham L. I. Daily State. Appendix III	16/05/1917	16/05/1917
Miscellaneous	20th Durham L. I. Daily State. Appendix IV	23/06/1917	23/06/1917
Miscellaneous	20th Durham L. I. Daily State. Appendix V	30/06/1917	30/06/1917
Miscellaneous	List Of Awards. Military Cross.	07/06/1917	07/06/1917
Miscellaneous	20th (S) Bn Durham L. Inf. Daily State.	07/07/1917	07/07/1917
Miscellaneous	20th (S) Bn Durham L. Inf. Daily State.	04/08/1917	04/08/1917
Miscellaneous	20th (S) Bn Durham L. Inf. Daily State.	21/08/1917	21/08/1917
Miscellaneous	20th Durham L. I. Daily State.	28/07/1917	28/07/1917
War Diary	In The Trenches.	01/08/1917	10/08/1917
War Diary	Ridge Wood	11/08/1917	12/08/1917
War Diary	Fountain Houcke	13/08/1917	20/08/1917
War Diary	Staples	21/08/1917	21/08/1917
War Diary	Esquerdes	22/08/1917	30/08/1917
War Diary	20th. Bn. Durham Light Infantry.		
Miscellaneous	20th Bn. Durham L. I. Daily State.	26/08/1917	26/08/1917
Miscellaneous	20th Bn. Durham L. I. Daily State.	19/08/1917	19/08/1917
Miscellaneous	20th Bn. Durham L. I. Daily State.	12/08/1917	12/08/1917
Miscellaneous	20th Bn. Durham L. I. Daily State.	05/08/1917	05/08/1917
War Diary	Esquerdes (Pas-de-Calais)	01/09/1917	14/09/1917
War Diary	Staple	15/09/1917	15/09/1917
War Diary	Phincboom	16/09/1917	16/09/1917
War Diary	Reninghelst (Albert Camp)	17/09/1917	18/09/1917
War Diary	Ridge Wood	19/09/1917	19/09/1917
War Diary	Hedge St	20/09/1917	20/09/1917
War Diary	Near Tower Hamlets	21/09/1917	23/09/1917
War Diary	Micmac Camp	23/09/1917	23/09/1917
War Diary	St Sylvestre Cappel	24/09/1917	26/09/1917
War Diary	Teteghem	27/09/1917	27/09/1917
War Diary	Zuydcoote	28/09/1917	30/09/1917
War Diary	In The Field	01/10/1917	01/10/1917
Operation(al) Order(s)	Operation Order No. 1.	03/09/1917	03/09/1917
Operation(al) Order(s)	20th Battalion Durham Light Infantry Operation Order No. 22. Appendix II	13/09/1917	13/09/1917

Operation(al) Order(s)	Operation Order No. 23.	14/09/1917	14/09/1917
Miscellaneous			
Operation(al) Order(s)	20th Bn. Durham Light Infantry Operation Order No. 25 Appendix V	18/09/1917	18/09/1917
Operation(al) Order(s)	20th Bn. Durham Light Infantry. Operation Order No. 26. Appendix VI	19/09/1917	19/09/1917
Operation(al) Order(s)	20th Bn. Durham Light Infantry. Operation Order No. 28. Appendix VII	25/09/1917	25/09/1917
Operation(al) Order(s)	20th Bn. Durham L. I. Operation Order No. 29 Appendix VII	26/09/1917	26/09/1917
Miscellaneous	20th Bn Durham L. I. Daily State.	01/09/1917	01/09/1917
Miscellaneous	20th Bn Durham L. I. Daily State.	15/09/1917	15/09/1917
Miscellaneous	Congratulatory Message.	22/09/1917	22/09/1917
Miscellaneous	20th Bn Durham L. I. Daily State	29/09/1917	29/09/1917
Miscellaneous	Congratulatory Messages		
Miscellaneous	20th Bn Durham L. I. Daily State.	08/09/1917	08/09/1917
War Diary	Zuydcote	01/10/1917	05/10/1917
War Diary	Stides Balde	06/10/1917	06/10/1917
War Diary	Trenches	07/10/1917	11/10/1917
War Diary	Middlesex Camp	12/10/1917	15/10/1917
War Diary	Bray Dunes	16/10/1917	31/10/1917
Map			
Miscellaneous	20th Bn Durham L. I. Daily State.	27/10/1917	27/10/1917
Operation(al) Order(s)	Operation Orders No. 75 by Capt. A. Mc. K. Reid, M.C. Commanding 123rd Company, M.G. Corps.	24/02/1918	24/02/1918
Miscellaneous	Table "A"		
Miscellaneous	O.C. 11th (S) Bn The Queen's Regt	18/06/1916	18/06/1916
Miscellaneous	20th Bn Durham. L. I. Daily State	20/10/1917	20/10/1917
Miscellaneous	20th Bn Durham. L. I. Daily State	13/10/1917	13/10/1917
Miscellaneous	20th Bn Durham. L. I. Daily State	06/10/1917	06/10/1917

41ST DIVISION
123RD INFY BDE

20TH BN DURHAM LT INFY

MAY 1916-~~FEB 1918~~ 1917 OCT

TO ITALY NOV 17

To 124 Bde

on Return from

ITALY

20 DLI
Vol 1
XLI

20th (SERVICE) BATTALION DURHAM LIGHT INFANTRY. 123rd INFANTRY BRIGADE.

W A R D I A R Y.

May 1916.
|
Feb 1918

Instructions regarding War Diaries and Intelligence Summaries are contained in F. S. Regs., Part II. and the Staff Manual respectively. Title Pages will be prepared in manuscript.

WAR DIARY
~~or~~
~~INTELLIGENCE SUMMARY~~
(Erase heading not required.)

Army Form C. 2118

20th (S) Bn Durham L. Infty

Place	Date	Hour	Summary of Events and Information	Remarks and references to Appendices
ALDERSHOT	MAY 4th	3.50am	The Battn entrained at FARNBOROUGH in three train loads at one hour's interval for the port of embarkation – SOUTHAMPTON. Strength, 34 officers 967 O.R. There were 4 absentees from Farewell Leave.	
SOUTHAMPTON.		6.30pm	30 Officers + 900 O.R. sailed for HAVRE on the S.S. Arundel arriving in HAVRE Harbour 12.45 a.m. 5.5.16.	
		7.30pm	Major Hills with the balance of the Bn + the whole of the Transport with other details sailed, arriving at HAVRE, 9 a.m. 5.5.16.	
HAVRE	5th	7.30am	Disembarked + marched to the Docks Rest Camp. Major Hills + his party joined at 5.0pm.	
"	6th	3.50am	The Battn, less "D" Coy, paraded + marched to the GARE DES MARCHANDISES. Left at 7.50 a.m. with the whole of the Transport for the front. Major Le Mesurier with "D" company followed with other details later.	
STRAZEELE	7th	7.30am	The Battn, less "D" Coy, detrained at GODESWAERWELDE and marched to billets at STRAZEELE, about 5½ miles, passing through the billeting area of the 50th Northumbrian + Durham Division whose Headquarters were at FLÊTRE.	
"	8th		Major Le Mesurier + his party detrained at HAZEBROUCK + joined the Battn at STRAZEELE. 2nd Lieut. J. E. Dixon + 12 O.R. left to form part of personnel of Brigade Bombing Company.	
"	9th		Lieut. C. E. Hopkinson appointed 123rd Inf. Bde Intelligence Officer.	
"	10th		The C.O., Adjutant, 5 Officers + 20 N.C.O.'s proceeded to trenches 90 – 93 in front of LE BIZET for an instructional tour in the portion of the line to be taken over by the Battn. They returned on the 12th inst. + a similar party of officers + N.C.O.'s proceeded for a tour. This continued until all officers + N.C.O.'s had spent two days in the trenches. The Signalling Officer + Battn Signallers also spent short periods in the trenches, learning the lines they were to take over. Corpl J. E. Norton (Lce Sergt) was slightly wounded by shell fire when with the first party.	
"	11th		Three O.R. left the Battn to take over Traffic Control Duties.	

1875 Wt. W593/826 1,000,000 4/15 J.B.C. & A. A.D.S.S./Forms/C. 2118.

Instructions regarding War Diaries and Intelligence Summaries are contained in F. S. Regs., Part II. and the Staff Manual respectively. Title Pages will be prepared in manuscript.

WAR DIARY

~~or~~

~~INTELLIGENCE SUMMARY~~

(Erase heading not required.)

Army Form C. 2118

20th (S) Bn Durham L. Infty.

Place	Date	Hour	Summary of Events and Information	Remarks and references to Appendices
STRAZEELE	MAY 12th		Sergt J. O. Elliot left the Battn to take up duties at the 41st Divisional Gas School.	
"	13th		Pte J. Hall, No 20/643 left to take over duties of Divisional Observer.	
"	16th		2nd Lieut. W. A. Rodwell & 35 O.R. left Battn & were attached to the 171st Tunnelling Company, R.E. They will eventually form part of the personnel of the 41st Divisional Tunnelling Coy.	
"	19th		8 O.R. detailed to form part of Divisional Pigeon Personnel (Signalling Section). The Bn & Transport were inspected by Lieut. General Sir Charles Fergusson, Bart. G.O.C. II Corps.	
"	21st		Lieut. H. Risdon left to take up duties as Adjutant & Quartermaster of the Divisional Trench Warfare School at NIEPPE.	
"	22nd		2nd Lt R. S. Green & 12 O.R. detailed as part of the personnel of the 123/1 Light Trench Mortar Batty	
	26th		31 O.Ranks ~~fo~~ left the Battn & were attached for duty to the Canadian Tunnelling Coy. at ARMENTIERES.	
"	27th	7.30am.	The Battn marched to NOOTE BOOM via MERRIS, 5½ miles, to billets	Weather very hot.
NOOTE BOOM	28th	2.30pm.	The Battn marched into Bde Reserve at LE BIZET, 9 miles, & came under ~~the~~ the command of the G.O.C., South African Brigade, taking over the billets of the 2nd S.A. Infty, which were little more than a heap of ruins.	
LE BIZET	29th		The Battn was rather severely shelled in LE BIZET during the afternoon. There were ~~6~~7 casualties (one slightly, at duty) among O.Ranks. Capt. E. Rasche admitted to hospital with severe burns on legs.	
		8.30pm.	Took over the trenches from the 1st S.A. Infty Trench map ARMENTIERES, 36 N.W. 2 Scale 1:10000. Trenches 91, 92, 93. Reserve at LE TOUQUET Station, & one platoon at LYS FARM. The 4th S.A. Infty on our left & the 17th Division on the right, South of the River LYS. The relief was carried out satisfactorily & expeditiously. Bn Hd Qtrs at SURREY FARM.	
LE TOUQUET STATION	30th		The first day in the trenches passed uneventfully. The 10th ~~11th~~ Bn Royal West KENT ~~Surrey~~ Regt took over from the 4th S.A. Infty on our left.	

Instructions regarding War Diaries and Intelligence Summaries are contained in F. S. Regs., Part II. and the Staff Manual respectively. Title Pages will be prepared in manuscript.

WAR DIARY

~~or~~

~~INTELLIGENCE SUMMARY~~

(Erase heading not required.)

Army Form C. 2118

20th (S) Bn Durham L. Infty

Place	Date	Hour	Summary of Events and Information	Remarks and references to Appendices
LE TOUQUET STATION	MAY. 31	1.30 am.	Casualties during night 30/31, Killed O.R. one ~~Wounded~~ wounded: O.R. one. Lieut. J. Thompson-Hopper went out twice to where they had been working with wiring party & carried in both men.	
		5 p.m.	The G.O.C. 123rd Inf. Bde took over the Sector from the G.O.C. S.A. Infty Bde.	
		7 p.m.	Casualty. wounded, O.R. one slightly, at duty.	
			The 23rd Battn Middlesex Regt arrived in ARMENTIERES & the 11th Battn Royal West Surrey Regt in LE BIZET. The whole Brigade is now in the area.	

K. J. W. Leather Lieut Colonel.
Commdg: 20th (S) Bn Durham Light Infty.

1875 Wt. W593/826 1,000,000 4/15 J.B.C. & A. A.D.S.S./Forms/C. 2118.

XLI

20 DLI
Vol 2
June

20th (SERVICE) BATTALION DURHAM LIGHT INFANTRY.

W A R D I A R Y.

JUNE 1916.

3rd Echelon

Army Form C. 2118

WAR DIARY
or
~~INTELLIGENCE SUMMARY~~
(Erase heading not required.)

20th (Ser) Battn Durham Light Infy

June 1916.

Instructions regarding War Diaries and Intelligence Summaries are contained in F. S. Regs., Part II. and the Staff Manual respectively. Title Pages will be prepared in manuscript.

Place	Date	Hour	Summary of Events and Information	Remarks and references to Appendices
In Trenches. (LE BIZET right Subsector Tr: 91, 92 & 93)	May 31st		Casualties: Wounded 1 O.Ranks. slightly, at duty. Capt: E. Rasche, sick, evacuated 30th May; invalided to England 31st May. (Strength State: June 1st: Total 34 officers 963 O.Ranks. Present with unit in Trenches 22 officers 696 O.Ranks. With Transport & Q.Master 1 officer 54 O.Ranks. Other Duties 11 officers 213 O.Ranks)	
— do —	June 2nd		Casualties: Lieut. J. H. Barker, Sniping Officer, badly wounded.	
— do —	JUNE 3rd.		Casualties: Killed. O.Ranks – One. Wounded: O.Ranks – One.	
— do —	4th		Casualties: Died of wounds: O.Ranks – One. The Battalion was relieved by the 23rd Bn Middlesex Regt. on the night of 4/5th. Went into rest billets in ARMENTIERES. One Company (supplying inlying picquet) went to the Laundry, LE BIZET. Relief complete, 1.20 a.m. 5th.	
ARMENTIERES	5th		The G.O.C. 41st Division congratulated the Battn on "the good work done in the trenches they occupied" (Copy attached).	
— do —	8th		Casualties: Wounded. O.Ranks – One: slightly, at duty. (Strength State: Total 32 officers 952 O.Ranks. Present with unit: 21 officers 752 O.Ranks. With Transport & Q.Master 2 officers & 61 O.Ranks. Other Duties 9 officers 139 O.Ranks).	
— do — In Trenches	10th		This Battn relieved the 23rd Bn Middlesex Regt. in trenches 91, 92 & 93. Relief complete, 10.50 P.M.	
In Trenches	11th		Casualties: Killed, O.Ranks, One. Wounded, O.Ranks 4.	
— do —	15th		Armourer Staff Sergt and draft of 31 O.Ranks arrived from base. (Strength State: not including above draft: Total 31 officers 933 O.Ranks. In Trenches 24 officers, 700 O.Ranks. Transport & Q.Master 2 officers 71 O.Ranks: Other duties 5 officers 162 O.Ranks. Wounded O.R. one.	

1875 Wt. W593/826 1,000,000 4/15 J.B.C. & A. A.D.S.S./Forms/C. 2118.

Instructions regarding War Diaries and Intelligence Summaries are contained in F. S. Regs., Part II. and the Staff Manual respectively. Title Pages will be prepared in manuscript.

WAR DIARY

or

~~INTELLIGENCE SUMMARY~~

(Erase heading not required.)

Army Form C. 2118

20th (S.) Bn Durham Light Infy

June 1916.

Place	Date	Hour	Summary of Events and Information	Remarks and references to Appendices
In Trenches ARMENTIERES	16th	—	This Bn was relieved by the 23rd Bn Middlesex Regt on night of 16/17th. Relief Complete at 1.0 am 17th. Proceeded to Rest Billet as on night of 4/5th.	
— do —	17th		Casualties: Killed: O. Ranks One.	
— do	22nd		(Strength State: Total 31 Officers 945 O. Ranks Present with unit in ARMENTIERES: 21 Officers 717 O. Ranks. With Transport & Q. Master 2 Officers 65 O. Ranks. Other Duties 8 Officers 163 O. Ranks.)	
— do —	23rd		Lt & Q. Master J. S. Simpkins – sick. Sent to Base. Capt W. W. Hiller took over duties.	
— do — In Trenches	24th		The Battn took over the Trenches (91, 92 & 93) from 23rd Bn Middlesex Regt. Relief Complete 12.4 a.m. 25th (Comm[on] Time).	
— do —	25th		Casualties: Wounded O. Ranks Two slightly at duty. Killed: O. Ranks One.	
— do	26th		" : Killed O. Ranks One. Wounded O. Ranks four.	
— do	28th		" : Wounded O. Ranks Two, both slightly at duty.	
— do	29th		Strength State: Total 31 Officers 931 O. Ranks. In Trenches: 22 Officers 701 O. Ranks. Transport & Q. Master 2 Officers & 69 O. Ranks. Other Duties: 7 Officers 161 O. Ranks.	
— do	30th.		Casualties: Wounded. Capt. M. Wayman. Lieut. J. Thompson-Hopper awarded Military Cross. Minor Operation "A" carried out (as per Bn O.O. No 9 attached) on 30th & night of 30.6.16/1.7.16. Casualties: Killed: Lieut. J. THOMPSON-HOPPER. O.R. two. Wounded: Capt. A. PUMPHREY, slightly at duty. O.R. ~~two~~ four. Suffering from shell shock – O.R. three, including 1 slightly at duty.	

K. J. L. [signature]

Lieut Colonel.

Commanding 20th (S) Bn Durham L. Infty.

1875 Wt. W593/826 1,000,000 4/15 J.B.C. & A. A.D.S.S./Forms/C. 2118.

S E C R E T.

With reference to Battalion O. O. No. 9 of the 27th inst.

1. The following code messages will be sent to inform all concerned which operation is to take place :-

" SEND TEST MESSAGE "A" " - Operation "A" to take place.

" SEND TEST MESSAGE "B" " - Operation "B" to take place.

The above messages will be sent out to Coy's. probably about 55 minutes before Zero hour. The time of the Zero hour will be sent to you as soon as received.

2. All lines connected with these operations will be kept clear of all except "Priority" messages from 8 p.m. 30-6-16.

J. Spencer Capt

30-6-16. Captain & Adjutant.

SECRET. COPY NO 8(a)

OPERATION ORDER NO 9
BY
LT.COL K.J.W.LEATHER, COMDG. 20TH BN DURHAM LIGHT INFANTRY.

27th June 1916.

Reference Secret Trench Map and Sheet 36 N.W. 2 I/IO,000.

I. Minor enterprises to capture prisoners and do as much harm as possible to the enemy will be carried out by the 20th Durham Light Infantry in conjunction with the IOth Royal West Kent Regiment. The Divisional Artillery, Trench Mortars and Stokes Guns will co-operate, and also the Brigade on the left of I23rd Infantry Brigade.

2. These enterprises will be either Operation A (with gas and smoke), to be carried out if the wind is favourable, or Operation B (without gas or smoke).

A message will be sent from Battalion Headquarters notifying the time of Zero, and a later message notifying whether Operation A or B is to be carried out.

3. OPERATION "A" (WITH GAS AND SMOKE).

BEFORE ZERO 45 MINUTES.

(a) Artillery will open fire for 30 minutes on portions of the hostile trenches from C.4.d.8½.3½. to a point to the N opposite the trenches held by the Brigade on the left of I23rd Infantry Brigade.

In the 20th Durham Light Infantry Subsector the following trenches will be subjected to intense bombardment, and the wire in front cut, viz:-

C.IO.b.4.4.

BEFORE ZERO 15 MINUTES.

(b) Artillery bombardment to cease for I5 minutes.

0.0. (ZERO HOUR).

(c) Gas to be discharged by personnel of Special Brigade R.E. from Trench 93 which will be cleared of other troops, and also from trenches 96 to IOI inclusive in the subsector of the IOth R.W. Kents Regiment.

0.1 MINUTE.

(d) Artillery will open a bombardment upon that portion of the hostile trenches mentioned in (a) above, making it intense at :-

C.IO.b.4.4.

0.2 MINUTES.

(e) Smoke to be discharged from Trench 93, bay 20 by 2nd Lieuts. Fletcher & Brown and I2 men of "D" Coy. Men to light and throw the smoke bombs and candles and to throw two smoke bombs and light one candle every minute until 0.23 minutes.

0.I5 MINUTES.

(f) Gas to be turned off. The personnel of the Special R.E. will use smoke candles in the bays containing gas emplacements from 0.I5 minutes to 0.25 minutes.

0.20 MINUTES.

(g) Trench Mortars to cease fire (see para 5).

From,
Headquarters,
20th Bn Durham Light Infantry.

To, Officer
i/c Adjutant-General's Office at the Base.

Herewith copy of War Diary for the month of June.

2nd July 1916.

Lieut. Colonel.

0.23 MINUTES.

(h) Artillery will lift from hostile front line trenches and will form barrages of fire behind and on either flank of C.10.b.4.4., communication trenches and lines of approach of reinforcements, also hostile batteries will be dealt with during this period.

0.28½ MINUTES.

(1) 2nd Lieut Britton with the patrol of II men already detailed will cross our parapet, advance straight to German lines, enter gassed locality opposite Trench 83, bomb dug-outs, capture one or two prisoners and report on effect of gas - remaining in the hostile trenches for IO minutes.

(2) This patrol will cross the parapet on the order of Captain Pumphrey, who will not give that order unless he is satisfied that the gas has had effect on the enemy trenches.

If after the patrol has started 2nd Lieut Britton sees that the enemy are lining their parapet and firing, the patrol will make their way back as best they can.

The IOth R.W. Kent Regt. will send out a similar patrol between C.4.a.8.2. and C.4.a.7.5.

The patrols are not to enter any hostile dug-outs and will wear their gas helmets rolled up on their heads.

During the time these patrols are out, the Infantry and Lewis Machine Guns in our Trenches on the flanks of the points of attack will maintain a brisk fire on the hostile trenches opposite them.

0.43 MINUTES.

All patrols will vacate the German Trenches. The Signal of recall will be given by 2nd Lieut Britton by whistle.

0.53 MINUTES.

Artillery bombardment ends.

2 HOURS 27 MINUTES.

There will be a second discharge of gas.

4. OPERATION "B" (WITHOUT GAS OR SMOKE).

This will be carried out by the IOth R.W. Kent Regt.

Para. 3 above (a) (b) (d) (g) & (h) will be carried out.

5. The Light Trench Mortars will co-operate in the Artillery bombardment under orders of the G.O.C. 123rd Infantry Brigade. They will only fire when the artillery is firing and cease at 0.20 minutes and not fire again. The Stokes Gun Battery will also cease fire at 0.20 minutes. No restrictions are placed on the rate of fire for Stokes Guns for this operation. O.C. this Battery or his Orderly will be at Battalion Headquarters at O.

6. All Identity Discs, and other marks of identification on clothing, equipment and arms, will be removed by the patrols.

All ranks taking part in the raid or patrols are to be warned that, if captured, they should give no information to the enemy, other than their name and rank.

7. These operations may provoke retaliation, and the Battalion is to be disposed so as to be as little vulnerable as possible to hostile shell fire. No working parties will be employed during the above operations.

8. All troops will take Gas Alert precautions as soon as the bombardment starts, (Before Zero 45 minutes) and all ranks must take special precautions that no one wearing the gas helmet at the "Alert" is visible to the enemy.

9. Lewis Gun Teams and Infantry firing to the flanks of the points being attacked, are to be careful not to mask the advance or return of the parties.

IO. If the operations are carried out at night, White tape is to be run out bt the party to mark the flanks and give a direction for return. Two guides to be set at gap in our wire.

II. As a great deal of wire will be cut during the morning of the day of the operation, the Infantry and Machine Guns in the front line will be responsible that they prevent the enemy sending out and repairing it, by continually firing into the wire at short intervals.

I2. Besides the other arms they carry, all patrols will be armed with a knob-kerry which will be slung round the wrist to prevent loss.

DETAIL OF OPERATION "A" WITH GAS AND SMOKE.

I. In the event of Gas and Smoke being used, Artillery Preparation and all orders appertaining to Operation "A" as detailed in Battalion Operation Order No 9 will be carried out.

A patrol as under will go out, and will bomb dug-outs, capture prisoners, do any damage they can, and report on the effect of our gas.

The party will consist of the following :-

Party - 2/Lt E.W. BRITTON and II Other Ranks, 20th D.L.I.

2. The party will leave our trenches from 93 trench at the hour stated. They will enter the German trenches at a point about C.IO.b.4.4. and will spread out, 5 men and a N.C.O. going to the left, 5 men and the Officer going to the right.

3. DRESS.

No equipment will be worn. Gas helmets will be worn at the "Alert". No dug-outs are to be entered. Every other man will carry a revolver, the remainder will be armed with a rifle and bayonet, one round in the chamber and 8 in the magazine, 25 in the pocket.

Revolver men will carry IO bombs in the Haversack slung round the waist, and men with rifles will have six bombs in the Haversack. Every man will have wire cutters.

4. RETURN SIGNAL.

At 0.43 2nd Lieut Britton will blow his whistle and the party will atbonce return to our own lines.

5. MEANS OF RETURN.

Two men will be placed at the openings of our own wire to guide the party back.

6. All members of this party will wear white diamond shaped distinguishing marks.

P. Spence

Issued at

Captain & Adjutant.

Copy No I Filed.
" " 2 O.C. A Coy.
" " 3 " B Coy.
" " 4 " C Coy.
" " 5 " D Coy.
" " 6 2nd Lt Fletcher.
" " 7 2nd Lt Britton.
" " 8 War Diary.

From,
Headquarters,
20th Bn Durham Light Infantry.

To,
Headquarters,
123rd Infantry Brigade.

In connection with the carrying out of B.O.O. No 6 and B.O.O. No 8 I beg to report as follows:-.

(a) ENEMY WIRE. There was practically no damage done to the enemies' wire. Out of 60 successive shots I only saw the wire hit once. This was not due to bad shooting but to the lay of the ground. The shooting was excellent and Major Whickham worked hard and most conscientiously the whole day up to 7.15 p.m. when we had a final look at the wire from our Salient and had to agree that it was not cut. The ammunition was most unreliable two or three shots out of five bursting over the support line, and the next two being perfect shots.

(b) DAMAGE TO ENEMY PARAPET. Very slight during wire cutting or afterwards.

(c) There was a perfect wind, and the gas and smoke floated well over the enemies' lines. My subaltern at LYS FARM reports that he saw the cloud for some distance back.

(d) Retaliation during wire cutting was very slight. The men lay on the duck boards, and although the parapet was hit in several places there were no casualties.

At 9.15 p.m. when our bombardment started, there was heavy retaliation within a minute. Every part of our trenches were treated, mostly shrapnel at first, later 4.2 and 5.9. As soon as our guns lifted the Germans guns shortened to No man's Land, and the parapet was manned. Converging machine gun fire from both flanks was very heavy from at least five or six guns.

(e) No identifications secured.

(f) Stokes guns fired 200 rounds per gun (4 guns).

Targets - German M.G. House, over Gap C, and the German Salient.

(g) POINTS BROUGHT TO NOTICE BY YESTERDAY'S OPERATIONS.
(1) Wire must be satisfactorily cut for a raid of this sort and the enemy M.G. emplacements treated severely with heavy shell.
(2) The enemy at once shortened their range and manned his parapet on our guns lifting.
(3) LONG AVENUE, NAPOO AVENUE & BARKENHAM AVENUE were all well treated with shrapnel throughout the bombardment.
(4) Red rockets were sent up, all along the German line, on our gas being discharged. Later single green rockets were sent up intermittently.
(5) 2nd Lieut Britton considers that it was too light when he went over the parapet.

As the wire had not been cut, it was impossible to carry out the raid planned, the wire being very thick in that place. 2nd Lieut Britton, however, volunteered to make for another point near the enemy salient where the wire looked weak. I consented to this but gave him strict orders to come back if he found the enemy wire too thick and the enemy parapet lined. When the time came for the raid our wire was quickly got through in file, but owing to the thick smoke the raiders could not be seen beyond this point until their return.

2nd Lieut Britton reports that the enemy wire consisted of knife rests two deep, and that he found the enemy parapet manned.

The casualties were slight owing to precautions taken. The men behaved splendidly and were quite unshaken by the bombardment, which was heavy.

Major Hills conducted operations from the first line and set a fine example to the men by his light-heartedness and pluck.

K. J. W. Leather.

1st July 1916. Lieut.Colonel.

July 1916 123/41

Instructions regarding War Diaries and Intelligence Summaries are contained in F. S. Regs., Part II. and the Staff Manual respectively. Title Pages will be prepared in manuscript.

WAR DIARY
or
~~INTELLIGENCE~~ SUMMARY
(Erase heading not required.)

41

Army Form C. 2118

20th (S) Bn Durham Light Infantry

VOL 3

Place	Date	Hour	Summary of Events and Information	Remarks and references to Appendices
Trenches 91-93 near LE BIZET.	JULY 1st.		Draft of 29 O.Ranks reported from 41st Div: Infty Base Depot. Remained at Transport Lines till 3rd. Casualties: wounded. O.R. Two.	Copy of Strength State attached.
— do —	2nd		Casualties: wounded 2/Lt Wayman (slightly, at duty). O.Ranks one. Battn was relieved by 23rd Bn Middlesex Regt on night of 2/3rd. One platoon of "A" Coy remained as Garrison of LYS FARM. Remainder of 'A' Coy went into billets at the Laundry, LE BIZET. The Battn, less A Coy, in billets at ARMENTIERES. Several buildings in ARMENTIERES on fire when Battn arrived. Fires caused by incendiary shells.	
ARMENTIERES.	3rd		Casualties: wounded. O.R. 4 including 2 slightly at duty. Suffering from Shell Shock. O.R. 2, "W".	
do	4th		" : Suffering from Shell Shock. O.R. one "W".	
do	5th		" : Suffering from Shell Shock. O.R. one "W"	
do.	6th		The line held by the Brigade was extended, the Battn holding the right subsector now holding from Gap A (Trench 90) to Trench 98. Remaining 3 platoons of 'A' Coy moved from billets in LE BIZET to the Subsidiary Line	
LE BIZET.	7th		The Battn, less A Coy, moved into Billets in LE BIZET, vacated by 10th Bn R. West Kent Regt. Casualties: One O.Rank died from wounds.	
— do —	9th		Casualties: wounded O.Ranks five	
— do —	12th		"B" Coy went to Divisional Lewis Gun School near BAILLEUL, for Special Training. Major Hills accompanied them as O.C. Enterprise. Capt. N.E.H. Sim attached to 123rd Inf. Bde for training in Staff Duties.	Copy of Strength State attached.
— do — & in Trenches (91 – 98)	14th		This Battn ~~of the~~ relieved the 23rd Middlesex Regt on the night of the 14/15. 'B' Coy remaining near BAILLEUL. One Company of Middlesex remained in Reserve at Le Touquet Station & the Company (less platoon) occupied the Subsidiary Line. One platoon Middlesex at LYS FARM. Distribution of Companies of this Battn as follows: "C" Coy Trenches 91 & 93 & Supports.	

1875 Wt. W593/826 1,000,000 4/15 J.B.C. & A. A.D.S.S./Forms/C. 2118.

July 1916.

Instructions regarding War Diaries and Intelligence Summaries are contained in F. S. Regs., Part II. and the Staff Manual respectively. Title Pages will be prepared in manuscript.

WAR DIARY
~~or~~
~~INTELLIGENCE SUMMARY~~
(Erase heading not required.)

20th (S) Bn Durham Light Infty

Army Form C. 2118

Place	Date	Hour	Summary of Events and Information	Remarks and references to Appendices
In Trenches.	14th		"B" Coy Trenches 93 & Supports. "A" Coy Trenches 96-98 & Supports. Trenches 94 & 95 (Gap 'C') patrolled by 'A' & 'B' Coys. Major F.H.S. Le Mesurier ordered to join his own regiment – the 1st Border Regt.	
— do —	15th		Casualties: wounded O.R. six, including 3 slightly at duty. Suffering from S. Shock, O.R. one "W".	Copy of Strength State attached.
— do	17th		Lt. G. Richwood, Transport Officer, sent to Hospital – sick.	
— do	19th		2nd Lts F.C. Arkless, H.B. Munro, J.O. Richardson, & F. Wilkin reported for duty. (from 23rd (R) Bn D.L.I.)	
— do	20th		Casualties: Killed, O.R. one. Missing O.R. two (from patrol). Wind ~~unfav~~ unfavourable for carrying out Bn Operation Order No. 12. (Copy attached).	
— do	21st		Casualties: Killed, O.R. one. Wounded, O. Ranks two.	
— do	22nd		Casualties: Wounded, Lt. Col. K.J.W. Leather, O. Ranks, four including 1 slightly at duty. 1 O. Rank released for munitions. Major J.W. Hills returned from BAILLEUL at 5 a.m. and took over the Command of Battn.	
— do —	23rd		The two O. Ranks reported missing on the 20th returned at 5 P.M. They had spent 3 days & 2 nights in "No Man's Land" between our trenches & the German trenches. Wire cutting had been carried out daily by our artillery & trench mortars. At night they could not find their way back. They came in during the time our 4.2 & 5.9 guns were bombarding the German trenches. Casualties: Killed O.R. one. This Battn was relieved by the 23rd Battn Middlesex Regt on night of 23/24. One coy less one platoon at LYS FARM, occupied the Subsidiary Line. Remaining 3 Coys & Head Qtrs went into Billets at LE BIZET. 'B' Coy still at Bailleul. Four O.R. attached to M.G. Company (permanently)	Copy of Strength State attached.

1875 Wt. W593/826 1,000,000 4/15 J.B.C. & A. A.D.S.S./Forms/C. 2118.

July 1916

Instructions regarding War Diaries and Intelligence Summaries are contained in F. S. Regs., Part II. and the Staff Manual respectively. Title Pages will be prepared in manuscript.

WAR DIARY

or

~~INTELLIGENCE SUMMARY~~

(*Erase heading not required.*)

20th (S) Bn Durham Light Infty.

Army Form C. 2118

Place	Date	Hour	Summary of Events and Information	Remarks and references to Appendices
LE BIZET.	26th		Enterprise as per attached operation orders was carried out of night of 26/27. Report on enterprise also attached + copy of letter from G.O.C. 41st Division. Casualties: killed O.R. 8 Missing, believed killed O.R. 4, wounded + missing O.R. one wounded 2Lt Britten + Capt. W. E. Jessop, latter slightly at duty. O.R. 50 including 5 slightly at duty suffering from shell shock, O.R. 7 "W"	
ARMENTIERES.	27th		The line held by the Brigade was readjusted, the Battn holding the right Inf sector being now responsible for Trenches 91 – 93. This Battn moved from LE BIZET to ARMENTIERES. The Coy in the Subsidiary Line came out into billets at the Laundry, LE BIZET, leaving one platoon as Garrison at LYS FARM. 2Lt W. P. M. Brettell proceeded to England on transfer to R. F. C.	
— do	28		2 other Ranks died from wounds received 26/27 July.	
— do	29		8 O. Ranks proceeded to join M. Gun Company (4 permanently + 4 for one month)	
— do	30th		One other rank reported "Missing believed killed" on 26/27 returned to trench 96 after spending 3 days + 3 nights in "No Man's Land". Casualties: wounded 2 O. Ranks, both slightly, at duty.	Copy of Strength State attached

[signature]

Major, Commanding

20th (S) Bn Durham Light Infty.

1875 Wt. W593/826 1,000,000 4/15 J.B.C. & A. A.D.S.S./Forms/C. 2118.

SPECIAL ORDER.

41 Div.
G.982.

123rd Inf. Bde.

The Divisional Commander desires you to have it made known to the 20th Bn Durham L.I. that he has noticed with satisfaction the good work done by the Battalion on the trenches they occupied. Both from what he has seen himself during his inspections of your line and from reports made to him, it is clear to him that all ranks have worked whole-heartedly at improving their breastworks, trenches and wire, while patrols and working parties at night have been active.

He desires you to congratulate the Battalion on the standard it has set for itself during its first tour of duty in the trenches.

(Sd) R. POPE HENNESSY.

4-6-16.

Major, G.S.

2.

To
O.C.,
20th Bn. Durham Light Infantry.

A/625.
4-6-16.

The G.O.C. in congratulating the O.C. 20th Bn. Durham L.I. on the well earned praise the Divisional Commander has bestowed on them, hopes that it may prove an incentive to all Battalions in his Brigade to endeavour to gain similar praise from all under whose command we may find ourselves from time to time.

(Sd) H.C.B.KIRKPATRICK.
Captain,
Brigade Major,
123rd Infantry Brigade.

1916.

20th (S) Bn. DURHAM LIGHT INFANTRY.

STRENGTH STATE.

	OFFICERS.	OTHER RANKS.
Present with Unit	21.	661.
Lys Farm	1.	44.
Armentieres		17.
Transport & Qr.Mr.Stores	2.	69.
Pigeon Personnel		2.
Attd to Div & Bde H.Q.	2.	25.
Attd to 171st Tunnelling Coy.	1.	51.
Attd to 250th -do-		29.
Traffic Control		1.
Bde Salvage Coy		2.
Div Training School	1.	1.
Hospital & Field Ambulances	1.	19.
Courses of Instruction		1.
Wounded	1.	-
Servant with Officer		1.
Attd to R.E.Nieppe.		2.
TOTAL.	30.	925.

Total Officers 30th - 31. 1 Officer Killed. Total 1st - 30
Total O.Ranks 30th - 931. 2 Killed. 3 Wounded. 1 Sick. evacuated. Total O.Ranks 1-7-16 - 925.

ATTACHED FOR RATIONS.

Trench Mortar Battery.	1.	11.
T.M.B. (Middlesex)	1.	20.
T.M.B. (Artillery)	1.	12.
Cemetery Keepers-2.Trench Wdns-3.		5.
TOTAL.	3.	48.

1-7-1916.

Lieut-Colonel.

20th (S) Bn. DURHAM LIGHT INFANTRY.

STRENGTH RETURN.

	OFFICERS.	OTHER RANKS.
Present with Unit	18.	588.
Subsidiary Trenches.	3.	110.
Lys Farm	1.	43.
Transport & Qr.Mr.Stores.	2.	64.
Pigeon Personnel		2.
Attd to Div & Bde H.Q.	2.	24.
Attd to 171st Tunnelling Coy	1.	53.
Attd to 250th -do-		26.
Attd to A.S.C.		2.
Traffic Control		1.
Bde Salvage Coy.		2.
Div Training School	1.	1.
Courses of Instruction		5.
Hospital & Field Ambulances	1.	20.
Attd to R.E.Nieppe.		2.
TOTAL.	29.	943.

Total O.R. 7th - 944. Evacuated 1. Total 8th - 943.

ATTACHED FOR RATIONS.

Trench Mortar Battery	1.	11.
Trench Wardens.		3.
2 Attd Middlesex. 1 A.S.C.		3.
TOTAL.	1.	17.

20TH (SERVICE) BATTALION 8 JUL. 1916 D 246 DURHAM LIGHT INFANTRY

8-7-1916. Lieut-Colonel.

20th (S) Bn. DURHAM LIGHT INFANTRY.

STRENGTH STATE.

	OFFICERS.	OTHER RANKS.
In Trenches.	15.	574.
At Lewis Gun School	6.	156.
Transport & Qr.Mr.Stores	2.	65.
Pigeon Personnel		2.
Attd to Div & Bde H.Q.	3.	24.
Attd to 171st Tunnelling Coy	1.	53.
Attd to 250th -do-		26.
Attd to A.S.C.		2.
Traffic Control		1.
Bde Salvage Coy		2.
Courses of Instruction		6.
Attd to R.E. Nieppe.		2.
Hospital & Field Ambulances		18.
TOTAL.	27.	931.

Total Officers 14th - 28. 1 Officer to Border Regt.
Total 15th - 27.
Total O.R. 14th - 936. 4 Evacuated. 1 To England (Munitions)
Total 15th - 931.

ATTACHED FOR RATIONS.

Trench Mortar Battery	1.	11.
5 Tramwaymen.2 Grave Diggers.		7.
TOTAL.	1.	18.

20TH (SERVICE) BATTALION 15 JUL. 1916 D383 DURHAM LIGHT INFANTRY

15-7-16. Lieut-Colonel.

20th (S) Bn. DURHAM LIGHT INFANTRY.

STRENGTH STATE.

	OFFICERS.	OTHER RANKS.
In Trenches	19.	549.
At Lewis Gun School	4.	164.
Transport & Qr.Mr.Stores	2.	72.
Pigeon Personnel		2.
Attd to Div & Bde H.Q.	3.	24.
Attd to 171st Tunnelling Coy	1.	53.
Attd to 250th -do-		26.
Attd to A.S.C.		2.
Traffic Control		1.
Bde Salvage Coy		2.
Courses of Instruction		8.
Attd to R.E.Nieppe		2.
Hospital & Field Ambulances	1.	14.
Servant with Officer		1.
Servant with Major Le Mesurier		1.
Missing		2.
TOTAL.	30.	923.

Total Officers 21st - 31. 1 Wounded. Total 22nd - 30.

ATTACHED FOR RATIONS.

Trench Mortar Battery	1.	10.
-do- (Artillery)	1.	14.
5 Tramwaymen, 3 Trench Wdns.		8.
4 Attd from R.A.M.C.		4.
TOTAL.	2.	36.

20TH (SERVICE) BATTALION 22 JUL. 1916 D573 DURHAM LIGHT INFANTRY

22nd July 1916. Lieut-Colonel.

20th (S) BN. DURHAM LIGHT INFANTRY.

STRENGTH STATE.

	OFFICERS.	OTHER RANKS.
Present with Unit	21.	569.
Lys Farm	1.	44.
Transport & Qr.Mr.Stores	1.	67.
Pigeon Personnel		2.
Attd to Div & Bde H.Q.	3.	24.
Attd to 171st Tunnelling Coy	1.	53.
Attd to 250th -do-		25.
Attd to A.S.C.		2.
Traffic Control		1.
Bde Salvage Coy		2.
Courses of Instruction		8.
Attd to R.E.Nieppe		2.
Hospital & Field Ambulances	1.	36.
Servant with Officer		1.
Attd to Machine Gun Coy.		4.
TOTAL.	28.	840.

RATIONED BY BATTALION.

Trench Mortar Battery.	1.	11.
3 Trench Wdms.2 Cemetery Keepers.		5.
TOTAL.	1.	16.

29-7-1916.

Major.

SECRET. COPY NO

20TH (S) BN DURHAM LIGHT INFANTRY. OPERATION ORDER NO. 12.

I. Provided the wind is favourable (W to S.W.) a surprise Gas Attack will be carried out by the personnel of "M" Coy, 3rd Bn. Special Brigade R.E. on the night July 20/21st from Trenches 93, 96, 97, 98, 100, 101, 102.
2. The bays of the above trenches will be temporarily cleared of Infantry during the discharge of gas. Any Sentry Posts left in the bays not containing cylinders will wear Gas Helmets.
3. Smoke will be discharged by the personnel "M" Coy, 3rd Bn. Special Bde R.E. simultaneously with the Gas from Tr: 92, 94, 95, 103, 104, 105.
4. All ranks in the front system of Trenches, between Trenches 91 & 98 (both inclusive) will take "Gas Alert" precautions.
5. No artillery, machine gun or rifle fire will be employed in connection with the Gas Attack.
6. The Zero hour for the attack will be between the hours of 12 midnight and 3 a.m. The actual time will be notified by wire by code word later.
7. Trenches cleared will be re-occupied at 0.30 mins.
8. Retaliation is to be expected, and all working parties must be warned to take cover.
9. Acknowledge.

July 20th 1916.

[signature]
Capt & Adjt.
20th Bn Durham L.I.

Code words to be used in this Operation.

ZERO	12 M.N.	Code	Henry I.
	12.15 a.m.		Henry II.
	12.30 a.m.		Henry III.
	12.45 a.m.		Henry IV.
	1.0 a.m.		Charles I.
	1.15 a.m.		Charles II.
	1.30 a.m.		Charles III.
	1.45 a.m.		Charles IV.
	2.0 a.m.		James I.
	2.15 a.m.		James II.
	2.30 a.m.		James III.
	2.45 a.m.		James IV.
	3.0 a.m.		William I.

Copy No 1 Filed.
" No 2 War Diary.
" No 3 O.C. "A" Coy. 20th D.L.I.
" No 4 " "C" Coy, "
" No 5 " "D" Coy. "
" No 6 " "A" Coy. 23rd Middlesex.
" No 7 " "B" Coy. "
" No 8 " Lys Farm Garrison.
" No 9 Machine Gun Officer.

SECRET. OPERATION ORDER NO 1 BY MAJOR HILLS, O.C. ENTERPRISE. Copy No

25-7-1916.

OBJECT. 1.- The object of the enterprise is to force an entry into the hostile front and support trenches in the RED HOUSE LOCALITY; to capture prisoners, machine guns etc., and destroy any mine shafts, dug-outs and emplacements encountered.

ALLOTMENT OF TROOPS. 2.- Right Blocking Party. Sgt Hanlon, 1 N.C.O., 4 Bayonet Men, 2 Bombers, 2 Carriers, 1 Sniper, 1 Worker. Total 12 O.R.

Left Blocking Party. Sgt Fletcher, 1 N.C.O., 3 Bayonet Men, 3 Bombers, 3 Carriers, 2 Workers. Total 13 O.R.

Right Assaulting Party. 2nd Lt.Fulljames, 4 N.C.O's, 7 Bayonet Men, 5 Bombers, 5 Carriers, 1 Runner 3 R.E: 3 R.E.Carriers.
Total: 1 Officer, 25 O.R., 3 R.E.

Left Assaulting Party. 2nd Lt.Britton, 4 N.C.O's, 5 Bayonet Men, 5 Bombers, 5 Carriers, 2 Runners, 3 R.E.: 3 R.E.Carriers.
Total: 1 Officer, 24 O.R., 3 R.E.

Covering Party. 1st Line. 3 N.C.O's, 24 Bayonet Men.
2nd Line. Capt.Jessop, Lieut.Carroll, 7 N.C.O's, 6 Bombers, 11 Bayonet Men, 6 Machine Gunners.
3rd Line. C.S.M.Walton, 2 N.C.O's, 4 Stretcher Bearers, 6 Tape Men, 4 Carriers, 4 Signallers.
1 Officer & 3 O.R. R.E. 3 R.E. Carriers.
Total 2 Officers, 81 O.R.
R.E. 1 Officer, 3 O.R.

Grand total 4 Officers, 155 O.R.
R.E.1 Officer. 9 O.R.

The Covering Party will supply the Advance Blocking Party consisting of : Cpl Jackson, 4 Bayonet Men, 4 Bombers, 4 Carriers : 13 O.R.

In addition to 4 Stretcher Bearers, all parties will carry some canvas stretchers.
Details of equipment are in appendix.

O.C.ATTACKING TROOPS. 3.- Capt Jessop is appointed O.C. Attacking Troops.

DATE & TIME. 4.- The date and zero hour will be communicated to all concerned.

WIRE CUTTING. 5.- Wire cutting by Artillery and Trench Mortars will be carried out on the front A B X (see plan attached) during the 48 hours prior to the enterprise. At the same time there are to be other "dummy" wire cuttings, notable at the Salient and opposite Trench 93-19.

TIME TABLE. 6.- 1 hour before Zero. Bombardments of points of attack by Heavy Artillery, Div.Artillery, Trench Mortars and Stokes Guns.
Counter Battery work by Heavy Artillery.

1 hour before Zero. Infantry leave our own trenches and form up on K-------------------------K

O.O. Zero hour. Bombardment lifts from hostile front line and barrages formed round localities to be attacked. Bombardment to continue on Enemy Support Trenches. Attacking Company advances from position of assembly (K--------------K) against the hostile trenches.

O. 10 min. Bombardment lifts from hostile Support Trenches and attacking parties as detailed will attack the enemy Support Trenches.

Barrages to continue until the O.C. Enterprise notifies Artillery that the party has returned to our trenches.

ACTION OF MORTARS.

7.- Stokes and Medium Trench Mortars will bombard the flanks of the LE TOUQUET and RAILWAY Localities and the N and N.W. face of the salient to prevent hostile machine gun fire from being brought to bear on the attacking party.

ACTION OF MACHINE GUNS. Trench 96.

8.- Machine gun fire will be brough to bear on top of enemy's parapet outwards from X^1 and X^2 and along the railway running through TWIN COTTAGES.

ACTION OF INFANTRY.

9.- The attacking party will leave our trenches as detailed and form up on line K-K in the following order:-

LEFT.	CENTRE.	RIGHT.
Blocking Party.	Covering Party.	Blocking Party.
Assaulting Party.		Assaulting Party.

The six tape men, will, as they go forward from our parapet, lay white tape to show the line, 2 men on right 2 in centre, and 2 on left.

The Signallers will run out a wire connected with O.C. Enterprise, along the centre tape.

(a) Blocking Parties.

The Blocking Parties covered by the covering Partyes as detailed in (b) will go over the parapet, the right party at A. the left at C and will block J & D. The 3 workers covered by a bayonet man and a bomber, will anchor the barbed wire "gate", firmly on the trench towards J & D respectively, and will construct a block towards A & C by pulling down sandbags etc. They will remain in position until recalled by O.C. Attacking Troops.

(b) Covering Party.

O.C. this party will detail tape layers as detailed. He will also detail two bombing squads (10 men each) to remain at A & C to support the two blocking parties if required. He will cover the entries of the Blocking Parties at A & C. He will protect the flanks in No Man's Land.

On the two blocks being completed, the Covering Party will thoroughly sweep trench A C, and occupy it, with its bombing arms. O.C. Attacking Troops will dispose of this party either in the trenches or behind the parapet as he thinks best, but will not himself cross the parapet. He will remain near point B in touch with his Signallers & runners. The Covering Party will remain in position until all other parties have left the hostile trenches. O.C. Attacking Troops is responsible for the recall of the left Assaulting Party, when the Right Assaulting Party have returned (see C) and for the recall of the Blocking Parties, when both Assaulting Parties have returned. He will then recall such of his party as are in trench A C, and will order the Demolishing Party to start work as detailed in (d). When all the Attacking Troops are clear of the hostile trenches, he will signal the return by coloured flares and bugle. He will immediately evacuate any wounded, prisoners, or war material captured.

(c) Assaulting Parties will act as follows :-

Left Assaulting Party. Moving in rear of the left Blocking Party, will be formed up in two parties, front and Support Line, the Officer being in rear of front line. They will move as quickly as possible to E. overland, unless impeded by wire. Arrived at E, they will block trench E M by pulling down sandbags and will await their supports who will work quickly up the trench C E, bombing dug-outs as they go. When the supports arrive at E The officer will leave a N.C.O. and 3 men at E and the whole party will work up trench E F as far as K, bombing dug-outs as they go and capturing prisoners and trophies. When recalled by O.C. Attacking Troops they will return by E C, picking up their party at E.

Right Assaulting Party. Moving in rear of the Right Blocking Party, will work up trench A H. Arrived at H, they will sweep trenches H G, G F & F B, bombing dug-outs and capturing prisoners and trophies. They will leave the hostile trenches at B, reporting there to the O.C.Covering Party, who will thereupon recall the Left Assaulting Party.

(d) Advanced Blocking Party. Will move at head of Right Assaulting Party and will block the Support Trench at H. They will be recalled by the same signal as the Left Assaulting Party and will return by H.A.

(e) Demolition Parties. Will take with them mobile charges for destroying mine shafts and deep dug-outs. Those attached to the Left Assaulting Party will leave their charges with a 5 minutes fuse on withdrawing down trenches K F C. Those attached to the Right Assaulting Party will similarly leave theirs as the party advances down H.G. G.F, F.B. Those attached to the Covering Party will similarly demolish trench A C, under orders of O.C. Attacking Troops when everyone has left or gone back to our own trenches.

(f) On reaching our trenches O.C. Enterprise will ascertain when all parties are back and will order the barrage to stop. No time limit is given, but time spent in the hostile trenches should not exceed 45 minutes.

MEDICAL. 10.- The M.O. will establish advanced Aid Post at a point to be arranged in LONG AVENUE. The M.O. 23rd Middlesex will be in attendance at the New Dressing Station in STATION AVENUE.

REPORTS. 11.- Headquarters will be in Gap C to which reports are to be sent. Lieut.Collins will be there and arrange for one signaller and two line repairers to attend. Artillery Liaison Officer will be there.

RENDEZVOUS.12.- All parties of whatever size will, on returning to our trenches, at once proceed by the shortest way to LE BIZET, first sending a runner to me in Gap C, giving the number and names of the party.

[signature]

Major.

Copy No 1 Filed.
" " 2 War Diary.
" " 3 G.O.C.
" " 4 O.C. Attacking Troops.
" " 5 M.O.
" " 6 Signalling Officer.
" " 7 O.C. Stokes Gun.
" " 8 O.C. Machine Gun Coy.
" " 9 O.C. 23rd Middlesex Regt.
" " 10 R.E.

APPENDIX.

EQUIPMENT FOR PERSONNEL.

Bombers. 12 Bombs (2 haversacks over each shoulder)
Revolvers - Knobkerries.

Carriers. Revolvers.
12 bombs (2 haversacks over each shoulder)
1 Bucket containing 20 bombs.
Knobkerries.

Bayonet Men. Rifle and Bayonet. (50 rounds S.A.A.)
6 bombs (1 haversack over each shoulder).

Wire cutters. One large pair of shear wire cutters, hedging gloves, slung rifle, (50 rounds S.A.A.) 6 bombs.

Laddermen. As for above except a 10' light ladder instead of wire cutters.

Signallers. Telephone and wire, electric lamp, revolvers, Signal bombs or lights.

Stretcher Bearers. Stretchers.
White tape.

Workers. Revolvers. One man to carry a pick, one a shovel, and to carry between them barbed wire "gate" for blocking trench. Third man to carry trench wire, mallet, 4 pickets or spikes, wire cutters.

R.E. Revolvers, 12 bombs, mobile charges.
Every man to have a clasp knife, and every Officer and a proportion of N.C.O's electric torches.

All men to carry clasp knives.
All revolver carriers to carry 24 rounds.

From,
O.C.
20th Bn Durham Light Infantry.

To,
Headquarters,
123rd Infantry Brigade.

Sir,

I have the honour to submit the following report on the Enterprise carried out on the night 26/27th:-

1. Our artillery started at 11 p.m. 26-7-16 and the attacking troops under my command consisting of 4 Officers and 155 Other Ranks, together with 1 Officer and 9 O.R. R.E., the whole under Capt Jessop, left our trenches according to programme and formed up on the line K---------K which I had had marked out the night before.

2. They were severely bombarded by the enemy artillery, chiefly with heavy H.E. shells, the bombardment being directed on No Man's Land in front of Gap C, for, though the parapet of Gap C was hit two or three times, and some shells went over it, the great majority fell between our own and the German trenches. This bombardment never lifted but continued in the same intensity until it ceased as stated in para. 6.

3. At 12 midnight Capt Jessop advanced and led his force to a disused trench just outside the German wire. He halted there to re-organise but found he had very few men with him. His own orderly, his tape layer and three of his four signallers had been killed or wounded. He therefore sent Lieut Carroll back towards our trenches to collect all the men he could, whilst he got in touch with his right and left. He found 2nd Lt Fulljames, commanding the Right Assaulting Party, who reported that he had lost touch with his Blocking Party (Sgt Hanlon), and feared that they had become casualties, and that the rest of his party had suffered heavily but that he had re-organised. Capt Jessop then returned to his position in the centre where he found Lieut Carroll, who had collected about 12 men. Capt Jessop could not get into touch with his left - 2nd Lt Britton.

4. Capt Jessop then advanced to the German wire. He found it uncut, consisting of knife rests covered with new wire. He was not fired at and saw no Germans. Considering it useless to attack with the few men that he had, he withdrew his force to the disused trench and came back and reported to me in Gap C.

5. Capt Jessop reached me at 12.30 a.m. and reported as above. I ordered him to withdraw at once to our trenches. At the same time I requested our artillery to stop the barrage and cease firing, for I anticipated that if our artillery ceased fire the German artillery would do the same, and that the attacking force could withdraw with greater safety. The anticipation proved correct. Our artillery ceased immediately and the German a few minutes later, except for one gun which fired five or six shells, and though German Machine Guns immediately opened a heavy fire, they fortunately caused no casualties either when the troops were returning or when they were bringing in our dead or wounded.

6. What remained of the attacking force reached Gap C shortly after 1 a.m. bringing all the wounded they could carry. I immediately organised parties to bring in the rest and No Man's Land was thoroughly searched. Fortunately it was a dark, misty morning, and we were enabled to continue work till between 3 and 4 a.m. By then I was satisfied that all the wounded were in and ordered work to cease. On the next night (27/28th July), I sent a party under 2nd Lieut Wayman to bring in some dead whom we had had to leave, and to make further search. He did this and brought in

two dead who had been clearly killed instanteously, and though he made a thorough search he could find no more.

7. The above accounts for all the Attacking Force, except the left under 2nd Lieut Britton and the Right Blocking Party. The left suffered very little from shell fire. At 12 midnight 2nd Lieut Britton advanced to the German wire. He found it completely flattened out, and was actually on the German parapet when he saw the recall signal. He thereupon withdrew and reached our lines without being molested. He found the trenches manned, and his party had begun to bomb them when recalled. Lieut Tandy, R.E. on 2nd Lieut Britton's right also reached the German parapet. He found the wire completely destroyed.

8. The Right Blocking Party under Sgt. Hanlon took up their position on K--------K as ordered. They were heavily shelled and lost some men. Accordingly Sgt. Hanlon moved them forward to escape shell fire, which he succeeded in doing. He advanced to a point not far from the German wire where they could see our shells bursting on the enemy's parapet. They escaped further casualties. At midnight they advanced to the German wire which they found uncut, new and old mixed together. The German trenches were manned. They could not get touch with anyone on their left. After waiting some time Sgt. Hanlon withdrew. In trying to reach our trenches, Sgt. Hanlon and four other men lost their way and wandered about till dawn, when they lay down and slept. During the day of the 27th July they crawled through the grass until they located Gap C. They returned to our lines about 7.45 p.m. bringing all their arms and equipment with them. One of the party was slightly wounded.

9. While I deeply regret that the Attacking Force failed to reach its objective, I consider that their failure was due to the very intense barrage to which they were subjected, and that no blame attaches to any Officer or man under my command.

10. All ranks without exception, behaved with great gallantry, coolness and devotion under the trying ordeal which they underwent. I am sending separately, the names of Officers, N.C.O's and men whose good conduct I beg to bring to your notice.

I have the honour to be,
Sir,
Your obedient Servant,

(SGD) J W HILLS.

Major,
Commdg 20th Bn Durham Light Infantry.

28th July 1916.

COPY.

To,
123rd Infantry Brigade.

Please convey to all ranks of the 20th Durham Light Infantry my congratulations on their gallant behaviour during the raid on the enemy last night. In face of the heavy barrage formed by the enemy's artillery, it was impossible to achieve the desired object, but all ranks deserve high praise for the soldierly spirit and gallant conduct which they displayed under severe fire.

(Sd) SIDNEY LAWFORD.
Major-General,
Commanding 41st Division.

To,
O.C.
20th Durham Light Infantry.

The above is a copy of a letter received by me from the Divisional Commander.

I fully endorse his remarks and would like all ranks to know that the Army Commander expressed his entire satisfaction with the result and conduct of the enterprise.

(Sd) C.S.DAVIDSON,
Brigadier-General,
Commanding 123rd Infantry Brigade.

July 28th 1916.

Instructions regarding War Diaries and Intelligence Summaries are contained in F. S. Regs., Part II. and the Staff Manual respectively. Title Pages will be prepared in manuscript.

WAR DIARY
or
~~INTELLIGENCE SUMMARY~~
(Erase heading not required.)

Army Form C. 2118

20th (S) Bn Durham Light Infy.

VOL 4

Place	Date	Hour	Summary of Events and Information	Remarks and references to Appendices
ARMENTIERES.	July 31st.		1 Other Rank reported as wounded and missing on July 27th returned to trenches of Battn occupying left sub sector.	
— do — and Trenches 91 – 95 (LE BIZET area).	AUGUST. 1st.		This Battn relieved the 23rd Bn Middlesex Regt on the night of the 1/2nd August. One platoon of Middlex Regt remaining as Garrison of LYS FARM. Casualties: Killed O.R. one.	
In Trenches.	2nd		Casualties: Wounded O.R. three, including two slightly at duty.	
— do.	3rd		Casualties: Wounded O.R. one.	
— do	5th		Casualties: Accidentally Killed: O.R. one. Wounded O.R. one.	
— do.	6th.		Casualties: Killed. O.R. one Wounded: O.R. four including two slightly at duty.	Copy of Str. State attached.
— do	8th.		Coys in support & reserve relieved coys in front line trenches. One Other Rank previously reported wounded 6.8.16 died of wounds. Strength Decrease: 3 O.Ranks proceeded to England for munition work.	
— do	9th		Casualties: Wounded O.R. two, including one accidentally.	
— do ARMENTIERES }	12th		This Battn was relieved by the 23rd Bn Middlesex Regt on the night of the 12/13th August. One Officer & 35 O.Ranks from 'C' Coy remained as Garrison of LYS FARM.	Copy of Str. State attached.
ARMENTIERES	14th.		Sir H. Plumer congratulated the Division on the splendid condition of the trenches they were leaving & spoke most warmly of the good work they had done. No. 27402 L/Cpl W.S. Smith & No 20/613 L/Cpl T. Cummings awarded Military Medal for gallantry on the night of the 26/27th July.	
— do —	15th		Casualties: Wounded O.R. one (Enemy shelling ARMENTIERES).	~~Copy of Str. State attached.~~
— do — and STEENWERCK }	16		This Battn was relieved in Rest Billets by the 13th Bn Durham Light Infty, part of 68th Infty Bde. The Battn marched to STEENWERCK & went into billets there for the night. Twelve O.Ranks rejoined from the 171st Tunnelling Coy.	
MONT DES CATS area }	17th		Battn marched to MONT DES CATS area & went into billets. Twenty two O.Ranks rejoined from 250th Tunnelling Company. A draft of 59 O.Ranks arrived from 35th Infty Base depot.	
— do —	18th – 22nd.		Battn in training. Route marches during the day. B.F. & P.T., Machine Gun destruction, Bombing &c in early morning and evenings.	Copy of Str. State for 19th attached.

1875 Wt. W593/826 1,000,000 4/15 J.B.C. & A. A.D.S.S./Forms/C. 2118.

Instructions regarding War Diaries and Intelligence Summaries are contained in F. S. Regs., Part II. and the Staff Manual respectively. Title Pages will be prepared in manuscript.

WAR DIARY
or
~~INTELLIGENCE SUMMARY~~
(Erase heading not required.)

Army Form C. 2118

20th (S) Bn Durham Light Infty

Place	Date	Hour	Summary of Events and Information	Remarks and references to Appendices
MONT DES CATS area	AUGUST. 20th.		No: 30231 Pte H. Lockey awarded Military Medal for gallantry on night of 26/27th July. One O. Rank proceeded to Base, under 19 years of age.	
BAILLEUL.	23rd.		The Battn marched to BAILLEUL and entrained there at 8.23 A.M.	
LONGPRE YAUCOURT-BUSSUS	24th	8.30am	The Battn detrained at LONGPRE les CORPS SAINTS (on the R. SOMME) and marched to billets at YAUCOURT-BUSSUS. (Ref: ABBEVILLE, 14, 1/100000).	
YAUCOURT-BUSSUS.	25th		Two drafts, of 60 and 80 O.R. respectively, arrived from 35th Infty Base Depot.	
— do —	29th		One O. Rank proceeded to base, under age. 2Lt J. Bainbridge (from 23rd (R) Bn D.L.I.) and 2Lt W. Mitchell, from 17th Bn D.L.I. reported for duty.	Copy of Str. State for 18th inst. attached.
— do —	26th to 30th.		Battn engaged in intensive training for the attack. From the 26th to 30th training much hampered by continuous & heavy rain.	

[illegible signature]
Lieut Colonel,
Commanding 20th (S) Bn Durham L. Infty.

1875 Wt. W593/826 1,000,000 4/15 J.B.C. & A. A.D.S.S./Forms/C. 2118.

WAR DIARY

20th DURHAM. L. I.

From Sept. 17th to Sept. 30th 1916

Instructions regarding War Diaries and Intelligence Summaries are contained in F. S. Regs., Part II. and the Staff Manual respectively. Title Pages will be prepared in manuscript.

WAR DIARY
~~or~~
~~INTELLIGENCE SUMMARY~~
(Erase heading not required.)

Army Form C. 2118

Vol 5.

20th (S.) Bn. Durham Light Infantry.

Place	Date	Hour	Summary of Events and Information	Remarks and references to Appendices
YAUCOURT BUSSUS	Sept. 1st		1 O.R proceeded to No. 2 Prisoners of War Camp RIBEMONT under age. Battalion Continued training for the attack from 1st to 5th inst.	Copy of Str. State atts.
do	" 2nd		Lieut. & Q. Master J.S. Simpkins returned to Battalion from England.	
do	" 3rd		2nd Lieut. R.M. Fulljames awarded Military Cross for gallantry on night of 26/27th July	
do	" 4th		1 O.R proceeded to Base for discharge. 1 O.R proceeded to No. 2 Prisoners of War Camp RIBEMONT under age.	
do	" 5th		Transport left by road for Forward Area.	
do / NEAR BECORDEL	" 6th		The Battalion marched from YAUCOURT BUSSUS to LONGPRE LES CORPS SAINTS and entrained there for MERICOURT. Arrived MERICOURT 8.30 p.m. and marched from there to Camp near BECORDEL. Ref. Map ALBERT 1/40,000 The transport arrived on the same day.	Copy of Str. State atts.
NEAR BECORDEL.	" 8th		1 O.R proceeded on Traffic Control Duties. Commanding Officer, Adjutant, Coy Commanders & 4 other officers proceeded to trenches on Tour of Inspection	
—do—	9th		Battalion moved to Camp 2,000 Yards Nearer firing line. 1 O.R proceeded on Munition Work	
do.	10th		1 O.R. do do.	
In trenches.	11th		The Battalion moved into Trenches in Support behind 11th Bn. 'Queens' Regt. and occupied CARLTON and SAVOY Trenches. Battalion relieved 7th Kings 165th Bde. Owing to congestion of trenches, one Coy moved to YORK TR. and one Coy to MONTAUBAN LINE. On night of 11/12th two Coys advanced the front line occupied by 11th Queens 100-150 yards by establishing a chain of posts 100 yards apart, and as far as possible connected up the posts and dug back Communication trenches to front line during the Night. The parties withdrew when it was too light to work without being observed with the exception of one Company which remained to hold the posts. Casualties:- Wounded. Lieut A.F. Collins. " O.R 8. Missing O.R. 1.	

1875 Wt. W593/826 1,000,000 4/15 J.B.C. & A. A.D.S.S./Forms/C. 2118.

Instructions regarding War Diaries and Intelligence Summaries are contained in F. S. Regs., Part II. and the Staff Manual respetively. Title Pages will be prepared in manuscript.

WAR DIARY
or
~~INTELLIGENCE SUMMARY~~

(Erase heading not required.)

20th (S) Bn. Durham L. I.

Army Form C. 2118

Place	Date	Hour	Summary of Events and Information	Remarks and references to Appendices
In Trenches.	12th		On night of 12/13th the Battalion relieved the 11th Queens in the front line. Queens moved into Support. Work on new Strong Point line continued & completed. Casualties. Lieut J.A. Struthers (Wounded). O.R. Wounded 16. Killed 4. Shell Shock W 3.	
do	13th		On night of 13/14th the Battalion was relieved by 15th Bn Hants Regt, 122nd Bde and moved back to trenches close to POMMIERS REDOUBT. Casualties. Wounded O.R 3. 2nd Lieut. J.O. Richardson to England.	
Nr. POMMIERS REDOUBT.	14th		Battalion rested during the day. 41st Division were detailed to attack & capture the Enemy's defences (including FLERS) up to including the line Pt N 20 d-5-0 (exclusive) - N. 20.c.3.6 - Road Junction N 25 b. 0.6. 123rd Bde was detailed as Divisional Reserve. At 12 midnight the Battalion moved to take up position in CHECK LINE from S.22.a.66 to S.22 b. 10.0. Casualties:- O.R. 6 Killed 16 Wounded. 1 Missing 2 Shell Shock "W".	Map Ref. Special Map. French Maps issued LONGUEVAL 57cSW.
CHECK LINE & ORIGINAL FRONT LINE.	15th		Attack Commenced 6.20 am. As the Attack proceeded the Battalion moved up & took over part of trenches from which the attack commenced. Casualties:- Wounded 2nd Lieut. F.C. Arkless. O.R. Killed 1. Wounded 35 Missing 2 Shell Shock "W" 6.	
ORIGINAL FRONT LINE.	16th		The Battalion moved to FLERS DEFENCES & remained there in reserve. During this move the Battalion passed through a heavy Enemy barrage & suffered fairly heavy Casualties. Wounded Capt. P. Spencer, Capt. D.E. Jessop, Capt. H. Rigdon, 2nd Lt. Wm. Fletcher. 2nd Lt. W. Mitchell, Lt. C.E. Hopkinson, 2nd Lieut. F. Wayman } Two latter Slightly At duty. Casualties:- O.R. Killed 6, Wounded 61, Wounded & Missing 2, Missing 7.	
FLERS DEFENCES	17th		The Battalion was relieved on night of 17/18th by 7th Bn King's & proceeded to MONTAUBAN LINE. Casualties:- O.R. Killed 2, Wounded 19. Wounded & Missing 1. Missing 5.	
	18th		Arrived MONTAUBAN LINE 5 am. Proceeded from there to Camp near BECORDEL.	
NEAR BECORDEL.	19th to 27th		Battalion took part in training for the attack. 25th Casualties. Wounded. O.R 1 (Accidently)	Copy of St: State for 22nd atto
- do -	27th		At 7pm. the Battalion moved to bivouac East of MAMETZ	
EAST of MAMETZ	28th		The 123rd Bde relieved 164th Bde & came under orders of 21st Division. This Battalion relieved 8th Kings Liverpool Regt. 2 Coys occupied SMOKE TR & 2 Coys FOSSEWAY (Near FLERS)	

1875 Wt. W593/826 1,000,000 4/15 J.B.C. & A. A.D.S.S./Forms/C. 2118.

Instructions regarding War Diaries and Intelligence Summaries are contained in F. S. Regs., Part II. and the Staff Manual respectively. Title Pages will be prepared in manuscript.

WAR DIARY
or
~~INTELLIGENCE~~ SUMMARY
(Erase heading not required.)

Army Form C. 2118

20th (Ser.) Bn Durham Light Infantry

Place	Date	Hour	Summary of Events and Information	Remarks and references to Appendices
IN TRENCHES.	29th		Quiet day save for Casualties to carrying parties to front line at Night. Casualties Killed O.R. 3. Wounded O.R. ten including three Sl. at duty.	
" "	30th		Two Companies of the Battalion relieved two Companies of the 11th Bn Queens in the front line Commencing at 2.30 pm. They were Evidently seen by the Enemy as heavy shell fire was the result & the remaining two Companies withdrew in accordance with orders received. D Company suffered heavy Casualties in going into the trenches. At 7.30 pm. the whole relief was completed, the remaining two Companies relieving the Queens in the Support & Reserve. Working parties were sent up from the two latter Companies to assist the Companies in the Front line in deepening & strengthening their trench which had been dug the previous night in front of [illegible] support, an old German trench. Casualties Killed O.R. Four. Wounded O.R. 31 including 5 Sl. at duty. Missing O.R. 3. Officers wounded. Lt Col J.W. Hills. Lieut C.E. Hopkinson.	

P. W. [illegible] Lt Col
O.C. 20th D.L.I.

1875 Wt. W593/826 1,000,000 4/15 J.B.C. & A. A.D.S.S./Forms/C. 2118.

20th (Ser) BN DURHAM LIGHT INFANTRY. 8-9-16.

STRENGTH STATE.

	OFFICERS.	OTHER RANKS.
Present with Unit.	27	894.
Pigeon Personnel.		3.
Attd to Div. and Bde H.Q.	1	12.
Attd 171st Tunneling Coy.	1	
Traffic Control.		2.
Attd to A.S.C.		2.
Bde Salvage Coy.		2.
Railway Operating Division. ANDRUICQ.		1.
Detailed to look after kit at STEENWERCK.		1.
Courses of Instruction.	1	5.
Servant with Officer.		1.
Hospital and Field Ambulances.		17.
Machine Gun Coy (Permanent).		8.
-do- (1 month).		4.
TOTAL.	30	951.

Total O.R. 7th - 950. 1 Sick Rejoined - Total 8th 951.

20th (Ser) BN DURHAM LIGHT INFANTRY - STRENGTH STATE. 2-9-16.

	OFFICERS.	OTHER RANKS.
Present with Unit.	26	932.
Transport & Qr.Mr. Stores	1	62.
Pigeon Personnel.		3.
Attd to Div. & Bde H.Q.	1	11
Attd to 171st Tunneling Coy.	1	-
Traffic Control.		1
Attd to A.S.C.		2.
Bde Salvage Coy.		2.
Divisional Observer.		1.
Courses of Instruction.		8.
Hospital & Field Ambulances.		26.
Attd to Machine Gun Coy. (Permanent.)		8.
-do- (1 month).		4.
TOTAL.	29	960

20th (Ser) Bn DURHAM LIGHT INFANTRY - STRENGTH STATE. 22-9-16.

	OFFICERS.	OTHER RANKS.
Present with Unit.	20	676.
Attd to Div.& Bde H.Q.	1	14.
Pigeon Personnel.		4.
Attd to A.S.C.		2.
Traffic Control.		2.
Hospital.		17.
Courses of Instruction.		3.
Railway Operating Division.		1.
Detailed to look after Kit.		1.
M.G.Coy (Permanent).		8.
-do- (Temporary).		4.
Bde Salvage Coy.		2.
Transport Lines &c.		[illegible].
Attd to 171st Tunneling Coy.	2	69.
	1	-
	24	803.

ATTACHED FOR RATIONS.

Trench Mortar Battery.	1	13.

Vol 6

CONFIDENTIAL

War Diary

of

20th. (S) Bn. Durham Light Infantry.

from Oct. 1st 1916 to Oct. 31st 1916, inclusive

Instructions regarding War Diaries and Intelligence Summaries are contained in F. S. Regs., Part II. and the Staff Manual respectively. Title Pages will be prepared in manuscript.

WAR DIARY
or
INTELLIGENCE SUMMARY
(Erase heading not required.)

Army Form C. 2118

20th (S) Bn. Durham Light Infy.

Place	Date 1916	Hour	Summary of Events and Information	Remarks and references to Appendices
Trenches in front of FLERS	1st Oct.		In the afternoon three patrols of 7 men and 1 N.C.O. went out behind a barrage while Brigades on our right and left were advancing. Their orders were to find out whether the enemy trenches in front were occupied or not and if they were they were ordered to dig in not nearer to them than 200x. In spite of very heavy Machine Gun, Rifle, and shell fire they did so and finding the trench occupied dug in some 200x from it and held out until relieved 7 hours later. The party was under an officer. At night the Battn. was relieved by the 8th Bn. Royal Fusiliers and went back to POMMIERS REDOUBT near MONTAUBAN. F.W. 2/Lt. Casualties:— Killed 2, Wounded 25, Missing 3.	1. Copy of Bgde Order attached.
POMMIERS REDOUBT	2nd Oct.		The Battn. remained in rest at POMMIERS REDOUBT. Major P.W. North from the 5th Bn. Royal Berkshire Regt. joined the Battn. to take over command. F.W. 2/Lt.	
MAMETZ WOOD	3rd Oct		In the afternoon the Battn. moved camp to a camp near MAMETZ WOOD. F.W. 2/Lt.	
	4th "		Remained in rest. F.W. 2/Lt.	
	5th "		Remained in rest and did some training. F.W. 2/Lt.	
	6th "		More training at same place. F.W. 2/Lt.	
	7th "		The Battn. received orders to proceed to SAVOY TRENCH as the 123rd Bde. were in Divisional Reserve while the other two Brigades were advancing. This we did and in the afternoon were ordered to go close up to SWITCH TR. We spent the night there. ~~and received~~ F.W. 2/Lt.	F.W. ~~2. Copy of Bgde Order attached~~
SWITCH TRENCH	8th "		SWITCH TRENCH is about 800x behind FLERS and this afternoon we were ordered to proceed to the front line to take over from ~~the~~ part of the 124th. Bde. They had not gained their objective but had dug in about 200x from the original front line.	2. Copy of Strength State attached.

1875 Wt. W593/826 1,000,000 4/15 J.B.C. & A. A.D.S.S./Forms/C. 2118.

Instructions regarding War Diaries and Intelligence Summaries are contained in F. S. Regs., Part II. and the Staff Manual respectively. Title Pages will be prepared in manuscript.

WAR DIARY
or
INTELLIGENCE SUMMARY
(Erase heading not required.)

Army Form C. 2118

20th. (S) Bn. Durham Light Infy

Place	Date	Hour	Summary of Events and Information	Remarks and references to Appendices
~~SWITCH TR.~~ FRONT LINE	8th (cont) Oct.		We relieved successfully and spent the night in ~~SWITCH TRENCH.~~ Front line FW. Casualties. NIL FW 2Lt	3. Copy of Bgde Order attached.
do.	9th. Oct.		A quiet day without much shelling. Improved the trenches and at night connected up two strong points which had been dug. F.W. 2Lt Casualties Killed O.R. 2 Wounded 5 Missing 1. FW 2Lt	
do	10th Oct.		At night commenced wiring the front line and succeeded in getting out much wire in spite of heavy M.G. and rifle fire. Later we were relieved by the 2nd Bedfordshire Regt. And came back to our old camp near MAMETZ WOOD. Casualties — Wounded. Officers 2Lt. J.W. Butterfield. Killed O.R. 1. Wounded 12 FW.	
MAMETZ WOOD	11th Oct.		Rested in camp. F.W. 2Lt	
	12th Oct		Trained and rested in camp. F.W. 2Lt.	
DERNANCOURT.	13th Oct		Moved back from camp to DERNANCOURT by train. FW. 2Lt.	
do	14th Oct.		Rested in DERNANCOURT FW 2Lt.	4. Copy of Strength State attached
do	15th		Inspected by Divisional General who presented Medal Ribbons to those who had gained distinction. FW 2Lt	
do	16th		Rested in DERNANCOURT. Transport left to go by road to CITERNE. FW 2Lt.	
	17th		Left DERNANCOURT at 2 pm. ~~and~~ to go to OISEMONT via AMIENS and LONPRÉ FW 2Lt	
CITERNE	18th		Arrived at OISEMONT and marched 3 miles to CITERNE where the Transport awaited us. Bn. H.Q. in the CHATEAU DE YONVILLE, a very fine country house, about one mile from CITERNE. FW 2Lt.	
CITERNE	19th.		Rested in CITERNE. FW 2Lt	

1875 Wt. W593/826 1,000,000 4/15 J.B.C. & A. A.D.S.S./Forms/C. 2118.

Instructions regarding War Diaries and Intelligence Summaries are contained in F. S. Regs., Part II. and the Staff Manual respectively. Title Pages will be prepared in manuscript.

WAR DIARY
or
INTELLIGENCE SUMMARY
(Erase heading not required.)

Army Form C. 2118

20th (S) Bn. Durham Light Infy.

Place	Date (Oct)	Hour	Summary of Events and Information	Remarks and references to Appendices
GODEWAERSVELDE	20th	–	Left CITERNE 12.15 a.m. and marched to PONT REMY where we entrained at 6 a.m. for GODEWAERSVELDE. Arrived there at 5 p.m. and were billetted on the outskirts of the town. J.W. 2/Lt	
— do —	21st		~~Left~~ Rested in GODEWAERSVELDE save for a party of officers who reconnoitred trenches in front of DICKEBUSCH J.W. 2/Lt	5. Copy of Stay of Stk attached
RENINGHELST	22nd		Left GODEWAERSVELDE ~~this~~ morning at 8.30 and marched to a camp at RENINGHELST. Here we were under canvas and spent the night of the 22nd there. J.W. 2/Lt. 2/Lt R.M. Fulljames awarded a Bar to Military Cross	6. Copy of Corps letter attached. XV
	23rd		Today we relieved the 49th. Bn. Australian Infy. in trenches in front of DICKEBUSCH. Relief carried out in daylight with no casualties. We marched to trenches via DICKEBUSCHE J.W. 2/Lt	
TRENCHES	24th		A quiet day. The trenches we hold are fairly good and at present are never shelled. The front line includes CRATER I and both it and the front line are very wet and require continually draining. The original support line is not held at all but we hold the old reserve line as our support and it is quite a good trench. No casualties today. J.W. 2/Lt	
TRENCHES	25th		Another quiet day. No Artillery fire on either side. Last night we wired a good deal of our front. Casualties NIL. J.W. 2/Lt	

Instructions regarding War Diaries and Intelligence Summaries are contained in F. S. Regs., Part II. and the Staff Manual respectively. Title Pages will be prepared in manuscript.

WAR DIARY *or* INTELLIGENCE SUMMARY

(Erase heading not required.)

Army Form C. 2118

10th (S) Bn. Durham Light Infy.

Place	Date Octr.	Hour	Summary of Events and Information	Remarks and references to Appendices
TRENCHES	26th		Today has been much livelier our Artillery being fairly active this morning. This afternoon the enemy put some Minenwerfers over so much so that retaliation was ~~fired~~ te wired for by the front line Coy. Commdr. This was immediately given with such good effect that the enemy was silent for the rest of the day. Today several officers of the 12th. E. Surrey Regt. who will probably relieve us soon, came up to reconnoitre the trenches. Capt. A Pumphrey went on leave to England. F.W. 2/Lt.	
			Casualties Killed O.R. 2 Wounded O.R. 3	
TRENCHES	27th		A very quiet day with showers of rain. No artillery activity	7. Copy of congratulatory letter from IV Army Commander attached.
			Casualties. Wounded O.R. 1. F.W. 2/Lt.	
do	28th		Another quiet day with several showers. Trenches very muddy.	
			Captain F.C. Chatt, previously of our Bn. re-joined for duty after serving with the 4th. Entrenching Bn.. 2/Lt. A.T. Browne and 2/Lt. H.K. Walton from the 4th Entrenching Bn. also reported in the trenches for duty today having reported at the Transport Lines yesterday	
			Casualties NIL. F.W. 2/Lt.	
do.	29th		Relieved in the afternoon and evening by 12th Bn. E. Surrey Regt. Relief entirely successful although carried out in daylight. The Bn. returned to camp at QUEBEC CAMP near RENNINGHELST	
			Casualties Wounded. O.R. 1. F.W. 2/Lt.	

1875 Wt. W593/826 1,000,000 4/15 J.B.C. & A. A.D.S.S./Forms/C. 2118.

Instructions regarding War Diaries and Intelligence Summaries are contained in F. S. Regs., Part II. and the Staff Manual respectively. Title Pages will be prepared in manuscript.

WAR DIARY
or
INTELLIGENCE SUMMARY

(Erase heading not required.)

20th (S) Bn. Durham Light Infy.

Army Form C. 2118

Place	Date	Hour	Summary of Events and Information	Remarks and references to Appendices
RENINGHELST	30th.		Rested and cleaned equipment etc. in camp all day. F.W. Lt.	
do.	31st.		Remained in Camp today. Roads and camp very muddy as is all the country in this vicinity. Most of the ground is under water and we receive frequent warnings etc. from Brigade and Division concerning Trench feet F.W. Lt.	

G. McNicall
Major
Commanding 20th Durham L.I.

1875 Wt. W593/826 1,000,000 4/15 J.B.C. & A. A.D.S.S./Forms/C. 2118.

(1)

SECRET.   Copy No 6.

123rd INFANTRY BRIGADE ORDER No. 34.

Reference Maps:- LONGUEVAL TRENCH MAP 57c S.W.3.
and Special Trench Maps.

1. The 123rd Infantry Brigade will be relieved by the 36th Infantry Brigade during the evening of the 1st, and night 1st/2nd October, in accordance with the attached relief table.

2. Each Coy. Commander will on relief hand over a sketch to the relieving Coy. Commander showing the exact distribution of his Coy., Lewis Guns and all information possible about his line.

3. The position to which the 123rd Infantry Brigade will march on relief will be notified later.

4. All details for taking over will be arranged by Commanding Officers concerned.

5. The 123rd M.G. Coy. Commander will report to Brigade Headquarters himself directly his relief is complete.

6. Very Pistols and periscopes will not be handed over on relief.

7. No unit is to leave its present position until relieved.

8. Completion of relief will be reported to Brigade Headquarter as follows:- "B.O.O. No.34 complied with".

9. Acknowledge.

(SGD) H.C.B.KIRKPATRICK.
Captain,
Brigade Major,
123rd Infantry Brigade.

September 30th 1916.

Issued to Signals at 8.15 p.m. 30-9-16 as under.

No. 1 Copy Filed.
No. 2 War Diary.
No. 3 11th Queens.
No. 4 10th R.W.Kent Regt.
No. 5 23rd Middlesex Regt.
No. 6 20th Durham L.I.
No. 7 2nd N.Z. Inf. Bde.
No. 8 110th Inf. Bde.
No. 9 36th Inf. Bde.
No. 10 21st Division.
No. 11 41st Division.
No. 12 123rd L.T.M.Battery.
No. 13 123rd M.G. Coy.
No. 14 Staff Captain.

20th (S) BN. DURHAM LIGHT INFANTRY. 2.

STRENGTH STATE.

	OFFICERS.	OTHER.RANKS.
For Trenches	18.	495.
Remaining	1.	50.
Transport Lines	1.	53.
Quartermaster Stores	1.	12.
Sick.		8.
Div & Bde H.Q.	2.	27.
Detached		7.
Bde Dump.		6.
Hospital		15.
Courses of Instruction		6.
Absent without leave		3.
Traffic Control		2.
Attd to A.S.C.		4.
23rd Divisional H.Qrs.		1.
Attd to Machine Gun Coy.		11.
Salvage Coy.		2.
171st Tunnelling Coy.	1.	–.
Pigeon Personnel.		7.
TOTAL.	24.	709.

ATTACHED FOR RATIONS.

From Royal Berkshire Regt.		1.
Machine Gun Coy.	1.	13.

7-10-16.

Lieut-Colonel.

20th (S) BN. DURHAM LIGHT INFANTRY.

STRENGTH STATE.

	OFFICERS.	OTHER RANKS.
Present with Unit.	21.	574.
Attd to Div & Bde H.Q.	1.	16.
In Hospital.	1.	20.
Pigeon Personnel		4.
Attd to M.G. Coy.		10.
" to A.S.C.		2.
" to 23rd Divl. J.Q.		1.
Salvage Coy.		2.
Traffic Control		2.
Courses of Instr.		5.
Absent without leave		3.
Detached at MEAULTE.	1.	50.
	24.	689.

ATTACHED FOR RATIONS.

T.M. Battery	1.	13.
From Berkshire Regt.		1.
	1.	14.

14-10-16.

Lieut-Colonel.

20th (S) BN. DURHAM LIGHT INFANTRY.

STRENGTH STATE.

	OFFICERS.	OTHER RANKS.
Present with Unit	13.	714.
In the trenches.	8.	20.
Attd to Div & Bde H.Q.	1.	14.
Absent with Leave	1.	–
In Hospital	1.	19.
Pigeon Personnel		4.
Attd to M.G.Coy.		10.
" to A.S.C.		2.
" 23rd Dibl. H.Q.		1.
Salvage Coy		2.
Traffic Control		2.
Absent without leave.		1.
TOTAL.	24.	789.

ATTACHED FOR RATIONS.

T. M. Battery.	1.	13.
From Berkshire Regt.		1.
From A.S.C.		2.
TOTAL.	1.	16.

21-10-1916.

Lieut-Colonel.

SECRET. Copy No 7.

123rd INFANTRY BRIGADE ORDER No.38.

1. The 123rd Infantry Brigade will be relieved by the 89th Infantry Brigade on the night of the 10/11th October 1916, in accordance with attached Relief Table.
2. One Officer per Coy. per Battalion in the Front Line, and one Officer per Battalion for Battalions in Support and Reserve, and 1 Offficer per Machine Gun Coy. and Stokes Mortar Battery will remain with relieving Battalions for 24 hours. Each of these observers will keep two observers with him for 24 hours, and all parties will rejoin their units near POMMIERS REDOUBT at the end of that time.
3. Trench Maps and Air Photographs will be handed over by Battalions.
4. Lists of code Orders, and Code Books for use with wireless &c. and copies of instructions for their use will not be handed over, but will be kept for further use.
5. Very Pistols and periscopes will not be handed over.
   Trench Mortars will be taken over in situ, but Vickers and Lewis Guns will be actually taken out of the line.
6. The observers who remain with the Officers for 24 hours will also be required to act as guides, and should therefore know their way about.
7. TURK LANE only will be used by this Brigade for relief, FISH LANE being allotted to 124th Infantry Brigade.
8. Brigade Report Centre will close at its present position on relief. All correspondence, except wires, should be sent to the Staff Captain near POMMIER REDOUBT after 9 p.m.
9. Completion of relief will be reported to Brigade Headquarters by wire by each unit, and by the T.M.Officer and M.G.Officer in person.
10. The Staff Captain will arrange for guides to meet Battalions on relief, between MONTAUBAN and POMMIERS, to guide them to their positions. Hot meals are to be ready, and Bivouacs pitched.
11. Acknowledge.

October 10th 1916.

(SGD) H.C.B.KIRKPATRICK.
Captain,
Brigade Major,
123rd Infantry Brigade.

Issued to signals at 10-10-16.

Copy No 1 Filed.
" No 2 War Diary.
" No 3 41st Division.
" No 4 11th Queens.
" No 5 10th R.W.Kent Regt.
" No 6 23rd Middlesex Regt.
" No 7 20th Durham L.I.
" No 8 123rd .M.G. Coy.
" No 9 123rd L.T.M. Battery.
" No 10.Staff Captain.
" No 11.89th Infantry Brigade.
" No 12.123rd Bde. Signalling Officer.

(6)

XV Corps A.C.1052/L.5.
41st Div. No. A.4/53.

41st Division.

Under authority granted by his Majesty the King, the General Officer Commanding-in-Chief has awarded decorations as shown below. Names which were submitted by you at the same time and which do not appear below, will be considered when the next Honours Despatch is being prepared. The recepients should be informed where possible. Their names will be published in the London Gazette in due course:-

BAR TO MILITARY CROSS.

2/Lieut. R.M.Fulljames, 20th Durham Light Infantry.

Headquarters,
22/10/16.

(signed) R.M.INGLE, Major,
D.A.A. & Q.M.G.

Headquarters,
123rd Infantry Brigade.

For information and communication to recipient. The Divisional Commander joins in the Congratulation of the Corps Commander.

(signed) G.F.Pragnell, Captain,
for Lieut.Colonel,
A.A. & Q.M.G.
41st Division.

2 th October 1916.

3.

O.C.
CHANGE.

For information and communication to recipient, please.

(signed) K.G.Livingstone. Lieut.
for Staff Captain,
GROTTO.

26th October 1916.

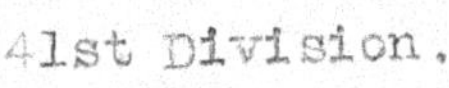

Fourth Army No. 355 (G.S).

41st Division.

I desire to place on record my appreciationof the work done by the 41st Division during the Battle of the Somme and to congratulate all ranks on the brilliant manner in which they captured the village of FLERS on September 15th. To assault three ~~strongly~~ lines of strongly defended trench systems, and to capture the village of FLERS as well, in one rush was a feat of arms of which every officer, non-commissioned officer and man may feel proud.

It was a very fine performance and I offer my best thanks for the gallantry and endurance displayed by all ranks.

The work of the Divisional Artillery in supporting the Infantry attacks and in establishing the ~~artillery~~ barrages deserves high praise, and I trust that at some future time it may be my good fortune to have this fine Division again in the Fourth Army.

(SGD) H.RAWLINSON.
General,
Commanding Fourth Army.

H.Q.4th Army,
27th October 1916.

41st Div.
G.454.

The Divisional Commander has great pleasure in forwarding the above. Such praise can only make all ranks proud of what they have done, and stimulate them to maintain in the future the name won by the 41st Division.

(SGD) B.L.ANLEY.
Lt.Colonel. G.S.

29-10-16.

48

Vol 7

Confidential

WAR DIARY OF

20th. (S). Bn. Durham Light Infantry.

from November 1st 1916 to November 30th 1916.

Army Form C. 2118

Instructions regarding War Diaries and Intelligence Summaries are contained in F. S. Regs., Part II. and the Staff Manual respectively. Title Pages will be prepared in manuscript.

WAR DIARY
or
~~INTELLIGENCE SUMMARY~~
(Erase heading not required.)

20th (S) Bn. Durham L. I.

Place	Date	Hour	Summary of Events and Information	Remarks and references to Appendices
RENINGHELST	1st Nov		The Battn. was inspected with the rest of the Brigade by General Sir H. Plumer G.C.M.G.K.C.B. Commanding the Second Army. In the afternoon did some training (Rifle Practice, Bombing etc) A new form of gas respirator was issued to the Battn. today. This is a lighter respirator than those previously in use and is supposed to be more effective. [initials] 2Lt.	
do.	2nd Nov.		Today instruction was given at the Divisional Gas School to the Battn. in the use of the new respirator. More Rifle Practice and Bombing done. [initials] 2Lt.	
TRENCHES	3rd "		Today we took over the same trenches that we were in last time. The relief commenced at 10.30 a.m. and we relieved the 12th. Bn. E. Surrey Regt. successfully in daylight. Weather quite good today and the ground much better than last week. The front line trenches are, however, still very dirty and are under water. Casualties – NIL [initials] 2Lt.	
–do–	4th.		A quiet morning but at 3.15 p.m. our guns commenced a fairly heavy bombardment on certain points in the enemy trenches. Practically no retaliation followed. [initials] 2Lt. Casualties NIL.	1. Copy of strength state attached.
–do–	5th		Another very quiet day. Practically no Artillery activity. The ground is growing worse as winter draws on and drainage presents a very difficult problem. The weather at present is, however, quite good and we suffer	

1875 Wt. W593/826 1,000,000 4/15 J.B.C. & A. A.D.S.S./Forms/C. 2118.

Instructions regarding War Diaries and Intelligence Summaries are contained in F. S. Regs., Part II. and the Staff Manual respectively. Title Pages will be prepared in manuscript.

WAR DIARY
or
~~INTELLIGENCE~~ SUMMARY
(Erase heading not required.)

Army Form C. 2118

Place	Date	Hour	Summary of Events and Information	Remarks and references to Appendices
	5th		no discomfort as yet. The wind has been blowing from N.E. to S for the last 3 days and as this is "dangerous" a "Gas Alert" has been on all the time. Casualties NIL. [illegible] 2/Lt.	
TRENCHES	6th		Very quiet again save towards evening. A raid took place on our right and much Artillery activity was observed. There was no retaliation on our sector, however. It is remarkable that the enemy rarely open fire here save in retaliation and their retaliation is very slight always. Obviously they suffer from lack of shells. Casualties Wounded O.R. 5 including 2 slightly at duty. [illegible] 2/Lt.	
—do—	7th		A very wet day today. Our trenches are so old that they will not stand the rain and in several places have fallen in. Several dug-outs have also suffered. Some of the trenches are flooded and require much work. Casualties NIL. [illegible] 2/Lt.	
—do—	8th		Weather finer today and the trenches are considerably drier. No artillery activity. Casualties Wounded O.R. 2 1 slightly at duty.	[illegible]
do	9th		Relieved today by 12th Bn. East Surrey Regt. Relief commenced at 10.30 a.m. and was completed by 4 p.m. We returned to ONTARIO Camp, a few yards away from our previous camping ground. Casualties NIL [illegible] 2/Lt.	

1875 Wt. W593/826 1,000,000 4/15 J.B.C. & A. A.D.S.S./Forms/C. 2118.

Instructions regarding War Diaries and Intelligence Summaries are contained in F. S. Regs., Part II. and the Staff Manual respectively. Title Pages will be prepared in manuscript.

WAR DIARY

or

~~INTELLIGENCE SUMMARY~~

(Erase heading not required.)

Army Form C. 2118

Place	Date	Hour	Summary of Events and Information	Remarks and references to Appendices
ONTARIO CAMP	10th		Trained in camp this morning and practised Musketry, Lewis Gunnery and Bombing on a miniature range which we have previously made. FW 2Lt.	
— do —	11th		Today was spent on the miniature range bombing, shooting etc. Inspected at work there by G.O.C. Brigade. FW 2Lt. Col. North went on leave today FW.	2. Copy of strength state attached
— do —	12th		Today G.O.C. Division presented ~~[illegible]~~ the medal ribbons to those who had gained them. Sergt. Winter and 2Lt. R.M. Fellowes were presented to him the latter having gained a bar to Military Cross and the former the Military Medal. FW 2Lt.	
— do —	13th		~~Trained at~~ The / All the Battalion were out on working parties today. The weather continues fine and roads and trenches are in good condition now. J. W. 2Lt.	
— do —	14th.		Trained at the range again all day. The men are now greatly improved in musketry, Lewis Gunnery, Bombing and Wiring. FW 2Lt	
— do —	15th		Trained in camp. FW. 2Lt.	
TRENCHES	16th.		Relieved the 12th. East Surrey Regt. in the trenches in front of DICKEBUSCH today. Relief commenced at 10.30 a.m. and finished at 4 p.m. Although the enemy must see these reliefs in daylight yet he never shells. The communication trenches are so open that ones head and shoulders show over the sides and	

1875 Wt. W593/826 1,000,000 4/15 J.B.C. & A. A.D.S.S./Forms/C. 2118.

Instructions regarding War Diaries and Intelligence Summaries are contained in F. S. Regs., Part II. and the Staff Manual respectively. Title Pages will be prepared in manuscript.

WAR DIARY
or
~~INTELLIGENCE SUMMARY~~
(Erase heading not required.)

20th (S) Bn. Durham L.I.

Army Form C. 2118

Place	Date	Hour	Summary of Events and Information	Remarks and references to Appendices
TRENCHES	16th		as the enemy hold the high ground they must see almost every movement. Casualties NIL J.W. 2/Lt	
— do —	17th.		A very quiet day today. The weather is now very cold and all the men have been issued with leather jerkins lined with cloth which are very warm and comfortable. All the men wear them as apart from being warm they also are rain proof. We have 10 Lewis Guns in the Battalion now, two new ones having been issued on the 6th. Inst. Casualties O.R. wounded 2 one slightly, at duty. J.W. 2/Lt	
— do —	18th.		Very cold today. Snow has fallen this morning and the duckboards were very wet and slippery. This afternoon, however, it has been raining and the trenches are exceedingly muddy now. Casualties Wounded O.R. 1. J.W. 2/Lt	3. Copy of strength state attached
— do —	19th		A very quiet day again today. Weather inclined to be showery and trenches very muddy. All available men are hard at work on the trenches endeavouring to repair them as they are in a very bad state. Casualties Nil J.W. 2/Lt	
— do —	20th		Wet again today. No artillery activity and no cases of "trenches foot" up to the	

1875 Wt. W593/826 1,000,000 4/15 J.B.C. & A. A.D.S.S./Forms/C. 2118.

Instructions regarding War Diaries and Intelligence Summaries are contained in F. S. Regs., Part II. and the Staff Manual respectively. Title Pages will be prepared in manuscript.

WAR DIARY
or
~~INTELLIGENCE SUMMARY~~

(Erase heading not required.)

Army Form C. 2118

Place	Date	Hour	Summary of Events and Information	Remarks and references to Appendices
TRENCHES	20th.		present. Casualties. Killed (Accidentally) O.R. 1 F.W. 2Lt.	
— do —	21st.		Weather finer today although the trenches are as wet as ever. Casualties Nil. F.W. 2Lt.	
— do —	22nd.		A fine day today. No enemy Artillery activity although every day our Artillery and Trench Mortars fire on the German Trenches. Retaliation rarely follows, however. Casualties Killed O.R. 1. F.W. 2Lt.	
ONTARIO CAMP.	23rd.		Relieved today by 12th. E. Surrey Regt. Relief commenced at 11 a.m. and was completed by 3.30 p.m. ~~The~~ The Battalion march back to ONTARIO CAMP near RENINGHELST which is composed of huts and is fairly comfortable. Casualties Nil F.W. 2Lt.	
— do —	24th.		Today has been spent in cleaning up. Everyone was very muddy yesterday and an entire day was required for purpose of cleaning clothes and equipment. Weather continues fine. F.W. 2Lt.	
— do —	25th.		Trained in camp. Weather wet. F.W. 2Lt.	4. Copy of strength state attached
— do —	26th		All the Battalion out on working parties today. F.W. 2Lt.	
— do —	27th		Trained in Camp all day. Ground very muddy and weather still wet. F.W. 2Lt.	

1875 Wt. W593/826 1,000,000 4/15 J.B.C. & A. A.D.S.S./Forms/C. 2118.

Army Form C. 2118

WAR DIARY
or
~~INTELLIGENCE SUMMARY~~
(Erase heading not required.)

Instructions regarding War Diaries and Intelligence Summaries are contained in F. S. Regs., Part II. and the Staff Manual respectively. Title Pages will be prepared in manuscript.

Place	Date	Hour	Summary of Events and Information	Remarks and references to Appendices
TRENCHES	28th Nov.		Relieved the 12th Bn. E. Surrey Regt. today. Relief commenced at 11 a.m. and carried out successfully without any casualties. Casualties NIL. [signature] 2/Lt.	
— do —	29th		A cold fine day today with thick fog. Our Artillery fired on hostile emplacements etc but no retaliation followed. Casualties NIL.	
— do —	30th.		Another cold day. Fog cleared. Artillery very active and much shelling took place, comprising Stokes Guns, M.T.M's. and Artillery. No damage was done however. Casualties NIL. [signature] 2/Lt.	

1875 Wt. W593/826 1,000,000 4/15 J.B.C. & A. A.D.S.S./Forms/C. 2118.

COPY. 20th (S) BN. DURHAM L.I. STRENGTH STATE.

	OFFICERS.	O.R's.
Present with Unit	16.	569.
At Transport Lines	2.	35.
Transport & Q.M.Stores.	1.	63.
Attd to Div & Bde H.Q.	3.	18.
Hospital.	2.	26.
Absent without leave		5.
" with leave	2.	3.
Attd to M.G.Coy.		10.
Camp Wardens.		2.
Traffic Control.		3.
Salvage Coy		3.
Attd to A.S.C.		2.
" " 250th Tunnelling Coy		10.
" " 1st Canadian " "		9.
" " 12th " " "		10.
" " R.E.		4.
Pigeon Personnel		6.
On Command		5.
Attd to 2nd Army H.Qrs.		7.
TOTAL	26.	790.

4-11-16.

2nd Lieut A/Adjt.
for Lieut-Colonel.

COPY. 20th (S) BN. DURHAM L.I. STRENGTH STATE.

	OFFICERS.	OTHER RANKS.
Present with Unit	15.	605.
Transport & Q.M. Stores	1.	68.
Attd to Div. H.Q.	1.	5.
Attd to Bde. H.Q.	2.	15.
Hospital	4.	36.
Absent without leave		1.
Absent with leave	2.	7.
Attd to M.G. Coy.		9.
Detention		2.
Attd to A.S.C.		2.
" " 250th Tunnelling Coy.		10.
" " 1st Canadian " "		9.
" " 12th " " "		9.
" " R.E.		4.
" " 233rd Field Coy	1.	13.
Pigeon Personnel		4.
On Command		11.
Salvage Coy		2.
Traffic Control		1.
2nd Army H.Qrs.		7.
Divl Guard.		12.
TOTAL	26.	832.

2nd Lieut. A/Adjt.
for Lieut-Colonel.

11-11-16.

COPY. 20th (S) BN. DURHAM L.I. (3) STRENGTH STATE.

		OFFICERS.	OTHER RANKS
In Trenches	x	16.	513.
Remaining behind			28.
Transport & Q.M.Stores		1.	66.
Attd to Div. H.Q.		1.	4.
Attd to Bde. H.Q.		2.	15.
Attd to 41st Divl. Train.			2.
Hospital		4.	~~38~~ 45
Absent without leave			1.
Absent with leave		3.	6.
Attd to M.G.Coy.			9.
Detention			2.
Attd to A.S.C.			2.
" " 250th Tunnelling Coy			10.
" " 1st Canadian " "			9.
" " 12th " " "			9.
" " R.E.			4.
" " 233rd Field Coy.		2.	25.
" " 123rd T.M.Battery			5.
Pigeon Personnel			6.
On Command			10.
Salvage Coy			2.
2nd Army H.Qrs.			7.
Traffic Control			1.
Divisional Guard.			12.
Brigade School			32.
Trench Warfare School			5.
x Includes 3 Offrs attd from OAR.		29.	832.

18-11-16. Lieut-Colonel.

COPY. 20th (S) BN. DURHAM L.I. STRENGTH STATE.

		OFFICERS.	OTHER RANKS.
Present with Unit	x	13.	523.
Transport & Q.M. Stores		1.	65.
Attd to Div H.Qrs.		1.	4.
Attd to Bde H.Qrs.		2.	15.
Attd to 41dt Divil. Train.			2.
Hospital		3.	61.
Absent with leave		2.	7.
Absent without leave			1.
Attd to M.G. Coy.			9.
" " A.S.C.			2.
" " 250th Tunnelling Coy			10.
" " 1st Canadian " "			9.
" " 12th " " "			9.
" " Divisional " "			32.
" " R.E.			4.
" " 233rd Field Coy.		1.	12.
Pigeon Personnel			3.
Salvage Coy.			2.
2nd Army H.Qrs.			7.
Traffic Control			1.
On Command		4.	27.
Base Prison			2.
T.M. Battery			2.
Brigade School			7.
x Includes 1 Offr. from OAR.		27.	816.

(SD) G. MCNICOLL Major,
For Lieut-Colonel.

25-11-16.

Instructions regarding War Diaries and Intelligence Summaries are contained in F. S. Regs., Part II. and the Staff Manual respectively. Title Pages will be prepared in manuscript.

WAR DIARY
or
~~INTELLIGENCE SUMMARY~~
(Erase heading not required.)

Vol 8 **Army Form C. 2118**

20th. (S) Bn. Durham L.I.

Place	Date	Hour	Summary of Events and Information	Remarks and references to Appendices
[T]RENCHES	DECEMBER 1st.		A quiet day. One of our patrols this morning bombed an enemy patrol and fired on them. 2/Lt. G. Frosty and 2/Lt. L. W. Stephenson took from the 10th. Entrenching Battn. reported for duty today. F.S. 2/Lt. Casualties — ~~Kil~~ Wounded O.R. 1.	F.S. 2/Lt.
— do —	2nd.		Another quiet day. Bad weather. No artillery activity. F.S. 2/Lt. Casualties NIL.	
— do —	3rd.		Relieved by 12th. Bn. E. Surrey Regt. Relief again took place in day light and was again successfull. Col. North went on leave to England today. F.S. 2/Lt. Casualties. NIL.	
ONTARIO CAMP	4th.		We are again back in Ontario Camp which is fairly comfortable. The Battalion has been out on Working Parties all day. F.S. 2/Lt.	
— do —	5th.		Cleaned up and repaired the camp today. F.S. 2/Lt.	
— do —	6th.		Trained in camp today. F.S. 2/Lt.	
— do —	7th.		All the Battn. at the Baths today. Training done in camp. F.S. 2/Lt.	
— do —	8th.		The whole Battn. on working parties again today. F.S. 2/Lt.	
	9th.		We relieved the 12th. Bn. East Surrey Regt. in the same trenches today.	

1875 Wt. W593/826 1,000,000 4/15 J.B.C. & A. A.D.S.S./Forms/C. 2118.

Instructions regarding War Diaries and Intelligence Summaries are contained in F. S. Regs., Part II. and the Staff Manual respectively. Title Pages will be prepared in manuscript.

WAR DIARY
or
~~INTELLIGENCE SUMMARY~~

(Erase heading not required.)

Place	Date	Hour	Summary of Events and Information	Remarks and references to Appendices
TRENCHES.			Relief successful and completed by 3 p.m. Casualties NIL. [illegible] 2/Lt.	
-do-	10th.		A quiet day. ~~No~~ Little artillery activity. Casualties. Killed O.R. 2 Wounded O.R. 2 [illegible] 2/Lt.	
-do-	11th.		Another quiet day. Weather wet and cold. The trenches are in a very bad condition at present and all available men are employed on their repair. Casualties NIL [illegible] 2/Lt.	
-do-	12th.		Weather still cold and wet. The enemy shelled our trenches a little but did no damage. [illegible] 2/Lt. Casualties NIL.	
-do-	13th.		A very quiet day. Weather warmer, still wet. Casualties NIL. [illegible] 2/Lt.	
-do-	14th.		Very quiet all day until about 9 p.m., when, after a short but heavy bombardment of Trench Mortars, the enemy raided the Battalion on our right. Result unknown. A few shells etc. were fired at us but no damage was done. At 7 p.m. today one of our patrols bombed an enemy machine gun with success. Casualties NIL. [illegible] 2/Lt.	
-do-	15th.		Relieved successfully today by the 12th Bn. E. Surrey Regt. Relief complete by 3 p.m. Back in ONTARIO CAMP by 5 p.m. Casualties NIL [illegible] 2/Lt.	

1875 Wt. W593/826 1,000,000 4/15 J.B.C. & A. A.D.S.S./Forms/C. 2118.

Instructions regarding War Diaries and Intelligence Summaries are contained in F. S. Regs., Part II. and the Staff Manual respectively. Title pages will be prepared in manuscript.

WAR DIARY
or
~~INTELLIGENCE SUMMARY.~~
(Erase heading not required.)

Army Form C. 2118.

20th Bn. Durham L.I.

Place	Date	Hour	Summary of Events and Information	Remarks and references to Appendices
	DEC.			
ONTARIO CAMP	16th		Cleaned up in Camp today. Weather very wet and camp very dirty and muddy. [illegible]	
— do —	17th.		Bn. on Church Parade in this morning. Did nothing save rest in the afternoon. [illegible]	
— do —	18th.		The Battn. on working parties all day today. Weather continues to be very wet and the roads, camps and parade grounds are very muddy. [illegible]	
— do —	19th.		The Battn. bathed, and practised Ceremonial Drill today. Horses inspected by the Divisional Commander. [illegible]	
— do —	20th.		Ontario Camp was inspected by the Divisional Commander today and he also inspected Companies training. [illegible]	
— do —	21st.		The Battn. paraded for inspection by the C. in C. today. The whole of the 123rd. Brigade was formed up in line along the RENINGHELST — OUDERDOM road. The C-in-C congratulated the battalion on its turn out and steadiness. A congratulatory letter was received from the Brigadier forwarding the remarks of the C-in-C and the Divisional Commander [illegible] 2nd Lieuts N.W.H. Cartwright, N. Southwell, & W.C.M. Stapleton reported from 3rd Bn. for duty.	
— do —	22nd		Battalion took over the trenches from 12th East Surrey Regt. Very quiet relief by day. [illegible]	
Trenches.	23rd		Quiet day. Two patrols were sent out by the battalion to patrol the enemy wire. Valuable information gained no opposition encountered.	

2353 Wt. W2544/1454 700,000 5/15 D. D. & L. A.D.S.S./Forms/C. 2118.

Instructions regarding War Diaries and Intelligence Summaries are contained in F. S. Regs., Part II. and the Staff Manual respectively. Title pages will be prepared in manuscript.

WAR DIARY

or

~~INTELLIGENCE SUMMARY~~.

(Erase heading not required.)

Army Form C. 2118.

20th Bn Durham L I

Place	Date	Hour	Summary of Events and Information	Remarks and references to Appendices
	Dec.			
Trenches.	24th		Quiet day. Weather, strong gale all day which died down at night. Wounded O.R 1 WHH Capt	
– do –	25th		Xmas Day. Certain amount of trench-mortar activity. Working parties etc as usual as we had been promised six days holiday when we go back to rest. Wounded O.R 1 WHH Capt	
– do –	26th		Quiet day. Two patrols went out from the battalion. Valuable information was gained about the enemy wire and No Mans Land by 2/Lieut Browne A Coy. Weather cold but fine rain towards evening.	
– do –	27th		Nothing of interest. Medium Trench Mortars bombarded the enemy trenches at two ~~expect~~ separate times during the day. A few 'minenwerfers' returned but no damages done. Wounded OR 1 WHH Capt	
– do –	28th		Normal day with frosty morning very wet at night. Heavy bombardment lasting about 5 minutes started on our right about 9 pm but nothing happened on our front. Wounded OR 1. WHH Capt	
– do –	29th		Bn relieved by the 12th East Surrey Regt. Relief took place by day with success but the relief of the CRATER was delayed owing to a hitch with Gumboots WHH Capt	
– do –	30th		Day spent in cleaning up and inspections under company arrangements. WHH Capt	
– do –	31st		Church parade in morning also demonstration at Brigade School. All officers & 150 O R were at the demonstration. Owing to an accident with a Stokes gun several casualties were incurred, 2/Lieut F. Wilkin and 2 O R being slightly wounded. The men had their Xmas	

2353 Wt. W2544/1454 700,000 5/15 D. D. & L. A.D.S.S./Forms/C. 2118.

Instructions regarding War Diaries and Intelligence Summaries are contained in F. S. Regs., Part II. and the Staff Manual respectively. Title pages will be prepared in manuscript.

WAR DIARY
or
INTELLIGENCE SUMMARY.
(Erase heading not required.)

Army Form C. 2118.

20th Bn Durham L I

Place	Date	Hour	Summary of Events and Information	Remarks and references to Appendices
Ontario Camp	31		Dinners at 1.30 pm the rest of the day being a holiday. The dinners were provided for out of a fund raised by the Mayor of Sunderland. HHS Capt	

P W North
Lt Colonel
Commanding 20th Bn Durham L I

Instructions regarding War Diaries and Intelligence Summaries are contained in F. S. Regs., Part II. and the Staff Manual respectively. Title pages will be prepared in manuscript.

WAR DIARY
~~or~~
~~INTELLIGENCE SUMMARY.~~
(Erase heading not required.)

Army Form C. 2118.

Vol 9 123/41

20th (S) Bn Durham L I

Place	Date 1917	Hour	Summary of Events and Information	Remarks and references to Appendices
	JAN			
ONTARIO CAMP	1st		Day spent in training and bathing. B.A went out to a hill where they practiced bombing, shooting & Lewis Gun. C Coy went to MICMAC and practiced bombing up a trench with dummy bombs. A Company were employed on building a new bombing ground near camp. MHS Capt	
-do-	2nd		The whole battalion employed on R.E. working parties MHS Capt. Wounded O R 1 MHS Capt.	
Trenches	3rd		The battalion relieved the 12th East Surrey regiment. The relief carried out by day again with success. Wounded O.R. 1 MHS Capt	
-do-	4th		Enemy's artillery and Trench Mortars were very active. Our trenches & communication trenches were knocked in at several places & portions of our wire cut. The night was spent in trying to repair some of the damage. Wounded O R 5 MHS Capt	
-do-	5th		Quiet day and night. Working party of 2 officers & 100 men sent to help us to repair the damage of the 4th. Some good work was done during the night. MHS Capt	
-do-	6th		Our medium Trench Mortars fired on the enemy trenches and wire from 2 30pm to 3 pm with apparently good effect. The Germans retaliated with artillery and trench mortars knocking our front line in at 8 places. The working party of 2 officers and 100 men again came to assist at night. Wounded O R 1 MHS Capt	

2353 Wt. W2544/1454 700,000 5/15 D. D. & L. A.D.S.S./Forms/C. 2118.

Instructions regarding War Diaries and Intelligence Summaries are contained in F. S. Regs., Part II. and the Staff Manual respectively. Title pages will be prepared in manuscript.

WAR DIARY
or
~~INTELLIGENCE~~ SUMMARY.
(Erase heading not required.)

Army Form C. 2118.

20th (S) Bn Durham L.I.

Place	Date	Hour	Summary of Events and Information	Remarks and references to Appendices
	1918 JAN.			
Trenches	7		A comparatively quiet day. A few shells fell round SUNDERLAND FARM where A Company were in reserve but no damage was done. 2 Officers and 100 men again came up at night. A patrol under 2/Lt W.O.M. STEPHENSON obtained useful information of enemy working parties. Killed O R 1. [initials] Capt.	
ONTARIO CAMP	8		Relieved by the 12th East Surrey Regiment during day. Relief successful. Very wet day with a strong wind blowing and the men got very wet returning to camp. Conference of all officers in the evening. [initials] Capt	
-do-	9		Day spent in baths, cleaning up, and medical inspection. The Army Commander (Sir Herbert Plumer) went round the camp in the morning but work was carried on as usual. [initials] Capt.	
-do-	10		The C.O inspected B Company at 10.30 am. After inspection B Coy went out for training. A Company threw live bombs at the Bn Bombing ground. C & D companies went to MICMAC to practice bombing with powder bombs. Commanding Officer lectured all officers in the battalion. 2/Lt B Wilkinson, 2/Lt W.R. Brooke, 2/Lt R. Jennings, 2/Lt P.L. Dobinson joined the battalion from 5th Training Reserve Bn. [initials] Capt	
-do-	11		All the Battalion employed on R.E. Working Parties. [initials] Capt	
-do-	12		The C.O inspected C Coy at 10.30 am. 40 of the worst shots of the Bn were trained under 2/Lt Walton at the Brigade Trench Warfare school. Companies carried out training in camp and on Bn Bombing ground. [initials] Capt	
-do-	13		Very wet day companies were unable to go out training. C.O. lectured all officers during the morning. Draft of 180 O.R. arrived from the 35th I.B.D. Orders were received that the Bn was to go into the trenches	

2353 Wt. W2544/1454 700,000 5/15 D. D. & L. A.D.S.S./Forms/C. 2118.

Instructions regarding War Diaries and Intelligence Summaries are contained in F. S. Regs., Part II. and the Staff Manual respectively. Title pages will be prepared in manuscript.

WAR DIARY
~~or~~
~~INTELLIGENCE SUMMARY.~~
(Erase heading not required.)

Army Form C. 2118.

20th (S) Bn Durham L.I.

Place	Date	Hour	Summary of Events and Information	Remarks and references to Appendices
	JAN.			
			a day earlier than was expected (14th). HHB Capt	
Trenches.	14th		Bn relieved the 12th R. Surrey Regt during the day. Relief carried out successfully. HHB Capt.	
-do-	15		Quiet day on the whole. Usual amount of hostile Trench Mortar activity. HHB Capt	
-do-	16		Normal day slight snow. Wounded OR 2 HHB Capt	
-do-	17		In the very early morning about 1am 2/Lt A. T. Browne took out a patrol to see if the enemy were alert after our wire cutting. The enemy were alert and threw bombs at the patrol. Snow fell fast all day the whole ground being covered. Wounded 2/Lt A. T. Browne and 1OR. The draft which had been left out of	
-			the trenches to undergo box respirator drill came up and took over SUNDERLAND FARM from D Coy 23rd Middlesex Regt who had been lent to us. 2/Lieut A.R. WILLIS from 4th H.L.I reported for duty. HHB Capt	
-do-	18th		Normal day. Snow still on the ground. The front line was twice bombarded by hostile Trench mortars and our artillery was called on for retaliation. HHB Capt	
-do-	19th		Enemy artillery very active. Shells fell in the neighbourhood of Bn Hqrs and SUNDERLAND HOUSE the latter being hit 6 times. All the men got out of the Farm before it was hit. HHB Capt	
-do-	20th		Very cold in the trenches owing to the snow being still on the ground. R Line was heavily shelled with 5.9 howitzers. One dug out completely blown in. Killed OR 2 wounded OR 3 HHB Capt.	
-do-	21st		The Battalion was relieved by 12th E. Surrey Regt. Owing to the snow the relief took place after dark. The relief	

2353 Wt. W2544/1454 700,000 5/15 D. D. & L. A.D.S.S./Forms/C. 2118.

Instructions regarding War Diaries and Intelligence Summaries are contained in F. S. Regs., Part II. and the Staff Manual respectively. Title pages will be prepared in manuscript.

WAR DIARY
~~or~~
~~INTELLIGENCE SUMMARY.~~
(Erase heading not required.)

Army Form C. 2118.

2nd Durham L I

Place	Date	Hour	Summary of Events and Information	Remarks and references to Appendices
			was carried out successfully. 2/Lt O.R. SHAW 2/Lt F.E.C.D. SMITH joined the battalion from the 3rd D.L.I.	HAS Capt
ONTARIO CAMP	22nd		The battalion were allotted the Baths, CHIPPEWA RANGE and the BRIGADE TRENCH WAFARE SCHOOL. All Lewis gunners armed with a revolver were given shooting practice at the Range. Each company had a turn at the trench warfare school. Instruction given was Rifle Grenade firing and Bayonet fighting. They were also shown different forms of loopholes. HAS Capt	
— do —	23rd		All the Battalion employed on R.S. Working parties. Weather still remained very cold with snow on the ground. HAS. Capt	
— do —	25th ~~24th~~		The Army Commander (Sir Herbert Plumer) inspected the battalion at Training. The C.O. held a lecture for all officers at 6 pm. HAS Capt	
— do —	24th ~~25th~~		Day spent in practicing OPEN WARFARE near MICMAC CAMP. The C.O. inspected the new draft which had arrived on the 13th.	
— do —	26th		All the battalion except "C" Coy were employed on R.E. working parties. C Coy practiced open warfare near MICMAC CAMP. The Divisional was expected to inspect "C" Coy but he did not. A draft of 118 OR and 6 Casuals arrived about 5 pm. The Commanding Officer inspected the draft before it dismissed. HAS Capt	
— do —	27th		CHIPPEWA RANGE was allotted to the Battalion. All companies fired "15 rounds a minute practice. Coys	

2353 Wt. W2544/1454 700,000 5/15 D. D. & L. A.D.S.S./Forms/C. 2118.

Instructions regarding War Diaries and Intelligence Summaries are contained in F. S. Regs., Part II. and the Staff Manual respectively. Title pages will be prepared in manuscript.

WAR DIARY

~~or~~

~~INTELLIGENCE SUMMARY.~~

(Erase heading not required.)

Army Form C. 2118.

[illegible] Capt

20th (S) Bn Durham L.I.

Place	Date	Hour	Summary of Events and Information	Remarks and references to Appendices
	Jan 1917			
			when not firing carried out bombing and open warfare training. [illegible] Capt	
ONTARIO CAMP	28th		Battalion relieved the 12th E. Surrey Regt. The relief took place by day. Weather dry and frosty and very cold. Snow still on the ground. Two patrols were sent out at night one under 2/Lieut JENNINGS and the other under 2/Lt BAINBRIDGE. Owing to the snow they were unable to obtain very useful information as they were observed in "no mans land" before reaching the german wire. [illegible] Capt	
Trenches	29th		Normal day. Snow still on the ground and hard frost day and night. Wounded OR 1 [illegible] Capt	
	30th		~~Quiet~~ Artillery & trench mortars active on both sides little damage done to us. Weather still very frosty. Killed OR 1 Wounded OR 2. [illegible] Capt	
	31st		Quiet morning but in the afternoon the enemy shelled the right front company with 5.9" whizzbangs also fishtail trench mortars. A Company suffered most having 1 man killed and 5 wounded. Total Casualties were Killed OR 3 Wounded OR 7 [illegible]	

[illegible] Lt Col.
O.C. 20th D.L.I.

20th. Bn. Durham. L. I. **STRENGTH STATE.**

	Officers.	O.R's.
Present with Unit.	15.	499.
Transport & Q. M. Stores.	1.	73.
Attd to Divl. H. Qrs.	1.	4.
" " Bde. "	1.	10.
Hospital.	2.	55.
Absent with leave.		3.
" without " .		1.
Attd to Royal Fusiliers.	1.	1.
" " A. S. C.		4.
" " 250th. Tunnelling Coy.		10.
" " 12th Chadaian Tunnelling Coy.		9.
" " Divisional Mining Coy.		4.
" " " Training School.		2.
" " 2[illegible]th Field Coy. R. E.	1.	15.
Hutting Work.		6.
Attd to R. E. ~~Spp~~ Poperinghe		4.
Musketry Instructor.		1.
Pigeon Personnel.		2.
On Command.	[illegible].	18.
Base Prison.		2
Brigade School.		7.
Divisional Fatigue.		5.
" Salvage.		1.
Attd to R. F. A.	1.	1.
Permanent Drainage Party.		2.
TOTAL.	51.	758.

15-1-17.

For Lieut: Colonel.
Comdg. 20th. Bn. Durham. L. I.

20th. Bn. Durham. L. I. STRENGTH STATE.

	Officers.	O.R's.
Present in Trenches.	21.	6[illegible]9.
Remaining Behind.	2.	[illegible]2.
Transport & Q. M. Stores.	2.	7[illegible].
Attd. to. Divl. H. Qrs.	1.	4.
" " Bde. " .		[illegible].
Hospital.	2.	5[illegible].
Absent with leave.	1.	1.
" without " .		1.
Attd to A. S. C.		[illegible].
" " 250th. Tunnelling Coy.		10.
" " 12th. Canadian Tunlg Coy.		9.
" " Divl Tunlg and Mining Coy.		4.
" " " Training School.		2.
" " 229th. Field Coy. R. E.	1.	1[illegible].
" " Hutting Work.		6.
" " R. E. Poperinghe.		[illegible].
Musketry Instructor.		1.
Pigeon Personnel.		[illegible].
On Command.	1.	26.
Base Prison.		2.
Brigade School.		7.
Divisional Salvage.		1.
" Fatigue.		[illegible].
Permanent Drainage Party.		2.
TOTAL.	31.	920.

20-1-17.

For Lieut: Colonel.
cmdg. 20th. Bn. Durham. L. I.

20th. Bn. Durham. L. I. STRENGTH STATE.

	Officers.	O.R's.
Present with Unit.	24.	75[illegible].
Transport & Q.M.Stores.	1.	70.
Attd. to Divl.H.Qrs.	1.	4.
" " Bde.	1.	10.
Hospital.	2.	2.
Attd to A. S. C.		4.
" " 250th. Tunnelling Coy.		10.
" " 12th.Canadian Tunnlg. Coy.		9.
" " Divl Training School.		2.
" " " Tunnlg and Mining Coy.		20.
" " 2[illegible]th. Field Coy. R. E.	1.	1[illegible].
" " R. E. Poperinghe.		4.
Absent with leave.	1.	
" without "		1.
Musketry Instructor.		1.
Pigeon Personnel.		[illegible].
On Command.		40.
Base Prison.		2.
Brigade School.	1.	[illegible].
Divisional Fatigue.		[illegible].
" Salvage.		1.
Permanent Drainage Party.		2.
Hutting Work.		[illegible].
Attd to Artillery Group.	1.	1.
	33.	1029.

[illegible]-1-17.

For.Lieut: Colonel.
Cmdg.20th. Bn.Durham.L.I.

20th. Bn. Durham. L. I. **STRENGTH STATE.**

	Officers.	O. R's.
In the Trenches.	19.	[illegible]
Remaining behind.		11.
Transport & Q. M. Stores.	1.	72.
Attd to Divl. H. Qrs.	1.	4.
" " Bde. "	1.	10.
Hospital.	2.	[illegible]
Absent with leave.		[illegible]
" without " .		1.
Attd to A. S. C.		4.
" " 250th. Tunnelling Coy.		10.
" " 12th Canadian Tunlg. Coy.		9.
" " Divisional Mining & Tunlg Coy.		[illegible]1.
" " " Training School.		2.
" " 2[illegible]th. Field Coy. R. E.	1.	12.
Hutting Work.		[illegible]
Attd to R. E. Poperinghe.		[illegible]
Musketry Instructor.		1.
At Dickebusch (Machine Gunners).		2.
On Command.	2.	[illegible]2.
Base Prison.		2.
Brigade School.		7.
Divl Fatigue.		[illegible]
" Salvage.		1.
Pigeon Personnel.		3.
	27.	7[illegible].

Lieut Colonel.

[illegible]-1-17. Comdg. 20th. Bn. Durham. L. I.

Instructions regarding War Diaries and Intelligence Summaries are contained in F. S. Regs., Part II. and the Staff Manual respectively. Title pages will be prepared in manuscript.

WAR DIARY
or
~~INTELLIGENCE SUMMARY.~~
(Erase heading not required.)

Army Form C. 2118.

February 1917 20th Durham Light Infantry.

Vol 10

Place	Date	Hour	Summary of Events and Information	Remarks and references to Appendices
TRENCHES	Feby 1st		Everything quiet today. Weather still cold and frosty. Casualties. Nil. Fw.	
— do —	2nd.		Another quiet day. Battalion working hard on the trenches all day. Casualties — Wounded O.R. 1. Fw 2Lt.	
— do —	3rd.		Battalion relieved by 12th Bn. East Surrey Regt in daylight and marched back to ONTARIO CAMP. Casualties O.R. 1. Fw 2Lt.	① Copy of strength state attached
ONTARIO CAMP ~~— do —~~	4th.		All Coys. fired rapid fire on CHIPPEWA RANGE, Lewis Gunners at range at Bgde. School and classes in camp. Fw 2Lt.	
— do —	5th.		All Coys at baths at Reninghelst after which they were inspected by the M.O. Training as usual was also carried out. Fw 2Lt. Lieut P.H. Coe reported for duty from 1st T.R.B.	2Lt.
— do —	6th.		Battalion all out on working parties in the neighbouring country. Fw 2Lt.	
— do —	7th.		Battalion route march in fighting order. Training in Artillery formation and open warfare. Fw 2Lt.	
— do —	8th.		Training in Lewis Gunnery, bombing, open warfare etc. Weather still very cold with no sign of a thaw. Fw 2Lt.	
— do —	9th		Battalion practiced in rapid fire, bombing, attacking etc. Fw 2Lt.	
do —	10th		Relieved 12th Bn. East Surrey Regt. in daylight successfully. Relief complete	

2353 Wt. W2544/1454 700,000 5/15 D. D. & L. A.D.S.S./Forms/C. 2118.

Army Form C. 2118.

Instructions regarding War Diaries and Intelligence Summaries are contained in F. S. Regs., Part II. and the Staff Manual respectively. Title pages will be prepared in manuscript.

WAR DIARY
or
~~INTELLIGENCE~~ SUMMARY.

(*Erase heading not required.*)

Place	Date	Hour	Summary of Events and Information	Remarks and references to Appendices
	Feby.			
TRENCHES.	10th.		by 2 p.m. Casualties – wounded O.R. 3. F.W.L.	(2) Copy of Strength State attached
– do –	11th.		Enemy Artillery very active today but little damage was done. Weather warmer but no thaw. Casualties O.R. wounded 1. F.W.L.	
do	12th.		Weather still warmer but not thaw yet. A quiet day. Casualties O.R. wounded 1. F.W.L.	
do	13th.		Weather still warm. Enemy very quiet but our Artillery active. Casualties Nil. F.W.L.	
do	14th.		Thaw commenced. Enemy still quiet. Casualties Killed O.R. 1. Wounded O.R. 1. F.W.L.	
do	15th.		Trenches very wet. Enemy more active but with no effect. Captain W. J. Hillier struck off strength (To England – sick). Casualties Nil. F.W.L.	
do	16th.		Our Artillery very active but enemy quiet. Casualties O.R. Wounded 1. F.W.L.	
ONTARIO CAMP.	17th.		Battn. relieved by 13th. Bn. East Surrey Regt. and marched back to ONTARIO CAMP. ~~7th~~ Casualties NIL. 2/Lieut. R.M. Upton and 2/Lieut. W.P. McGibbon from the 4th Bn. Durham L.I. reported for duty. F.W.L.	(3) Copy of Strength state attached
– do –	18th.		Battn. inspected by Commanding Officer. One Company at Church. Remainder rested all day.	
– do –	19th.		Battn. in working parties in the vicinity of the camp. Snipers, Lewis Gunners, and Buglers trained near camp. F.W.L.	

2353 Wt. W2544/1454 700,000 5/15 D. D. & L. A.D.S.S./Forms/C. 2118.

Instructions regarding War Diaries and Intelligence Summaries are contained in F. S. Regs., Part II. and the Staff Manual respectively. Title pages will be prepared in manuscript.

WAR DIARY
or
~~INTELLIGENCE SUMMARY.~~
(Erase heading not required.)

Army Form C. 2118.

Place	Date	Hour	Summary of Events and Information	Remarks and references to Appendices
ONTARIO CAMP	February 20th.		Half the Battn at the Baths, RENINGHELST, and half at the camp at CHIPPEWA CAMP. Usual training was carried out. [illegible]	
— do —	21st.		Exactly the same programme of work was carried out as yesterday. Weather wet and ground very bad. Roads muddy and surrounding country very wet [illegible]	
— do —	22nd.		Relieved the 12th. Bn. East Surrey Regt. in the trenches. Relief complete by 2 p.m. Trenches in a very bad condition. They are not damaged by shell fire much but are falling to pieces owing to the rain and thaw. Wounded. O.R. 1 [illegible]	
TRENCHES.	23rd.		Our Artillery very active today and enemy retaliated a good deal. No damage done, however. Casualties – Nil. [illegible]	
— do —	24th.		Today a raid was carried out by the 10th. Bn. Royal West Surrey Regt. in the 122. Brigade. The 26th. Bn. Royal Fusiliers are on our right and then the former Bn. hold the line. The whole of the Battn. raided at 5 p.m. in the daylight with good results. 1 officer and 53 O.R. are reported captured and more are coming down. We assisted the raid by sending up with	

2353 Wt. W2544/1454 700,000 5/15 D. D. & L. A.D.S.S./Forms/C. 2118.

Instructions regarding War Diaries and Intelligence Summaries are contained in F. S. Regs., Part II. and the Staff Manual respectively. Title pages will be prepared in manuscript.

Army Form C. 2118.

WAR DIARY
or
~~INTELLIGENCE SUMMARY.~~
(Erase heading not required.)

Place	Date	Hour	Summary of Events and Information	Remarks and references to Appendices
	February			
TRENCHES	24th (continued)		rockets from 4.30 p.m. to 5.5 p.m. The enemy shelled our trenches heavily at 4.30 p.m. evidently suspecting that we were raiding. Our front line was cleared, however, and we suffered few casualties. The front line was very badly damaged and the main communication trench (P and O) was badly blown in. Casualties Killed O.R. 4 Wounded O.R. 5. [initials]	(4) Account of patrol attached. (5) Copy of Strength state attached [initials]
— do —	25th		Artillery of both sides active today. All our men are employed in repairing the trenches which damaged yesterday. Weather fine. Casualties O.R. Wounded 9	
— do —	26th		A quiet day. Weather much finer and clearer. Trenches still in a bad condition, however. Casualties — NIL [initials]	
— do —	27th		Early this morning a patrol was sent out to endeavour to discover a working party (enemy) after first arranging a code word with the Artillery. An enemy working party was discovered in the enemy trench and at a fixed time the Artillery opened fire on it with field guns while Very Lights were put up from the front line and Lewis Gun and rifles fired on the party which could plainly be seen. Otherwise a quiet day. We were relieved by the 12th Bn. E. Surrey Regt. today. Casualties Wounded O.R. 1. [initials]	

Army Form C. 2118.

Instructions regarding War Diaries and Intelligence Summaries are contained in F. S. Regs., Part II. and the Staff Manual respectively. Title pages will be prepared in manuscript.

WAR DIARY

or

~~INTELLIGENCE SUMMARY.~~

(Erase heading not required.)

Place	Date	Hour	Summary of Events and Information	Remarks and references to Appendices
ONTARIO CAMP	February 28th.		Two and a half Companies out on working parties. Remainder training in Camp. Weather good. [illegible]	
			[illegible] Lt. Col. O.C. 2nd D.L.I.	

2353 Wt. W2544/1454 700,000 5/15 D. D. & L. A.D.S.S./Forms/C. 2118.

4

Account of Patrol on the night 24/25 February 1917.

A patrol of 6 men under Sergt. Winter left our trenches at 11.15 p.m. and discovered the whereabouts of a strong enemy working party. The patrol returned and heavy fire was brought to bear on the enemy party. Later, the patrol went out again to attempt to discover the extent of the enemy's losses. They encountered a German Patrol and a fight ensued in which Sergt. Winter and a private soldier was killed and another wounded. ~~The enemy are thought to have suffered some casualties.~~ Wounded men and dead bodies were brought in ~~and~~ Sergt. Winter was seen to bayonet one of the enemy before returning to his party mortally wounded himself.

[signature illegible]
Adjutant
[illegible]

20th Durham Light Infantry. (1) STRENGTH STATE.

	OFFICERS.	OTHER RA[NKS]
Present with Unit	26.	731.
Transport & Q.M.Stores.	1.	75.
Attd to Divl. H.Qrs.	1.	4.
" to Bde "	1.	10.
Hospital		48.
Attd to A.S.C.		4.
" " 250th Tunnelling Coy.		9.
" " 12th Canadian " "		9.
" " Divl.Tunlg & Mining Coy.		26.
" " " Training School		2.
" " 228th Field Coy. R.E.	1.	13.
" " R.E. Poperinghe.		4.
Absent with Leave.	1.	-
Absent without leave.		1.
Musketry Instructor.		1.
Pigeon Personnel.		3.
On Command		47.
Base Prison		2.
Brigade School	1.	8.
Divisional Fatigue		5.
" Salvage		1.
Permanent Drainage Party		2.
Hutting Work		6.
Traffic Control Duty.		1.
Y.M.C.A. DICKEBUSCH.		1.
TOTAL.	32.	1013.

For Lieut-Colonel.

3-2-17. Comdg. 20th Durham L.I.

A/555.

20th Durham Light Infantry. STRENGTH STATE.

	OFFICERS.	O.R's.
Present with Unit In Trenches.	22.	666.
Transport & Q.M. Stores.	1.	73.
Attd to Divl. H.Qrs.	1.	4.
" to Bde H.Qrs.	1.	10.
Remaining Behind.	1.	20.
Hospital.	3.	42.
Attd to Machine Gun Coy.		2.
" " A.S.C.		4.
" " 250th Tunnelling Coy.		10.
" "12th Canadian Tung. Coy.		9.
" " Divl. Tunlg. & Mining Coy.		25.
" " " Training School.		2.
" " 228th Field Coy. R.E.	1.	13.
" " R.E. Poperinghe.		4.
Absent with Leave	1.	1.
" without Leave		1.
Musketry Instructor.		1.
Pigeon Personnel.		3.
On Command.		55.
Base Prison.		1.
Brigade School.	2.	8.
Divisional Fatigues		5.
" Salvage.		1.
Permanent Drainage Party.		2.
Hutting Work.		6.
Traffic Control Duty.		1.
Divisional Guard.		8.
Buglers Remaining behind.		16.
TOTAL.	33.	992.

10-2-17.

A/599.

for Lieut-Colonel.
Comdg. 20th Durham L.I.

20[illegible] Durham Light Infantry. STRENGTH STATE.

	OFFICERS.	OTHER RANKS.
Present with Unit.	19.	733.
Transport & Q.M.Stores.	1.	69.
Attd to Divl. H.Qrs.	1.	4.
" " Bde "	1.	10.
Hospital.	4.	38.
Attd to Machine Gun Coy.		2.
" " 12th Canadian Tunlg.Coy.		9.
" " 250th Tunnelling Coy.		10.
" " Divl.Tunlg & Mining Coy.		25.
" " 228th Field Coy. R.E.	1.	12.
" " A.S.C.		4.
" " Divl. Training School.		2.
" " R.E. Poperinghe.		3.
Absent with leave		1.
" without leave.		1.
Musketry Instructor.		1.
Pigeon Personnel.		3.
On Command.	2.	23.
Brigade School.	2.	9.
Divisional Fatigue.		5.
" Salvage.		1.
Permanent Drainage Party.	1.	3.
Hutting Work.		6.
Traffic Control.		1.
TOTAL	32.	975.

17-2-17.

A/674. for Lieut-Colonel.
Comdg. 20th Durham L.I.

20th Durham Light Infantry. STRENGTH STATE.

	OFFICERS.	OTHER RANKS
Present in Trenches with Unit	21.	619.
At Transport Lines (Sick)		8.
Transport Section.	1.	56.
Quartermasters Establishment.		7.
Second Army.		2.
Xtg Corps H.Qrs. R.E's.		3.
Divisional Employ.	2.	12.
Brigade Employ.		10.
Attd to A.S.C.		4.
" " L.T.Mortar Battery.		1.
" " Machine Gun Coy.		5.
" " Divisional Tunlg. Coy.		22.
Brigade School.	2.	9.
Musketry School.		2.
Attd to 228th Field Coy. R.E.	1.	13.
" " 250th Tunnelling Coy.		10.
" " 12th Canadian Tunlg. Coy.		9.
Details left at Camp.		19.
Courses of Instruction.	2.	79.
Hospital.	4.	45.
Traffic Control.		1.
Pigeon Personnel.		3.
Drainage Party.	1.	3.
Absent without leave.		1.
Hutting Work.		6.
Attd to Camp Commandants Dept.		1.
Buglers remaining behind.		17.
Boxing Tournament.		1.
On Leave.		1.
TOTAL.	34.	969.

24-2-17. For Lieut-Colonel.

A/723.

Instructions regarding War Diaries and Intelligence Summaries are contained in F. S. Regs., Part II. and the Staff Manual respectively. Title pages will be prepared in manuscript.

20th Durham Light Infantry

WAR DIARY
or
~~INTELLIGENCE SUMMARY.~~

(Erase heading not required.)

for the Month of MARCH 1917

Army Form C. 2118.

Vol XI

Place	Date	Hour	Summary of Events and Information	Remarks and references to Appendices
	March			
ONTARIO CAMP	1st		Usual training under Company Arrangements, one company training at the Brigade School. Weather fine but misty. G.A.S. Lt Col	
-do-	2nd		Half the Battalion at the Baths RENINGHELST, the other two companies route marching under Company Arrangements. Weather misty some rain. G.A.S. Lt Col	
-do-	3rd		Battalion on working parties. At 4.30 pm a boxing competition was held in the Camp. Weather misty but fine in evening. G.A.S. Lt Col	① Copy of Strength state attached
-do-	4th		Church parade at the Y.M.C.A. hut RENINGHELST for C.E.s & Non Conformists and at the Parish Church RENINGHELST for R.C.s in morning. Inter Coy. football matches after church parade in the afternoon. A Coy beat B Coy 2-1. & A Coy beat D Coy (final) 8-2 weather fine. G.A.S. Lt Col	
TRENCHES.	5th		Relieved 12th E. Surrey Regt. Relief completed by 2 pm. Very quiet day. Weather:- Snowed during night but thawed in the day. Visibility very poor. G.A.S. Lt Col	
-do-	6th		Very quiet day. Weather fine but misty. Casualties nil. G.A.S. Lt	
-do-	7th		Quiet day. Weather very fine but cold. 2/Lt E. W. Brittin, who was previously with this Bn, reported for duty also 2/Lt. A Brown. Casualties 1 O.R. killed. G.A.S. Lt	
-do-	8th		Quiet day. Enemy raided trenches of 16th Division about 3000x ½ one night.	

2353 Wt. W2544/1454 700,000 5/15 D. D. & L. A.D.S.S./Forms/C. 2118.

Instructions regarding War Diaries and Intelligence Summaries are contained in F. S. Regs., Part II. and the Staff Manual respectively. Title pages will be prepared in manuscript.

WAR DIARY
or
INTELLIGENCE SUMMARY.
(Erase heading not required.)

Army Form C. 2118.

20 DLI
Vol

Place	Date	Hour	Summary of Events and Information	Remarks and references to Appendices
	March			
TRENCHES.	8th (cont)		Weather fine but misty. Casualties nil. G.A.S. 2/Lt	
-do-	9th		Very quiet day. Weather fine. Casualties. 2 O.R. wounded G.A.S. 2/Lt	
-do-	10th		Quiet day. Weather very misty. Casualties. 2 O.R. ~~gas~~ G.A.S. 2/Lt	(2) Copy of strength state attached.
-do-	11th		The Battalion was relieved by 12th E. Surrey Regt. The relief was completed by 2.4 pm. Casualties 2/Lt W.O.M. Stephenson slightly wounded. O.R. nil. G.A.S. 2/Lt	
ONTARIO CAMP	12th		Battalion on working parties. The Battalion Officers mess started at Dinner last night after many months waiting. G.A.S. 2/Lt	
-do-	13th		Battalion at Baths half at RENINGHELST & half at CHIPPEWA. Football match in afternoon. Officers beat the Sergeants 5–1. G.A.S. 2/Lt	
-do-	14th		Battalion training. Coys went out in different directions along roads & practised attacks &c. Cookers were taken. G.A.S. 2/Lt	
-do-	15th		Demonstration at Gas School in morning. Training under Coy arrangements in afternoon. A Boxing Competition was held in the afternoon. G.A.S. 2/Lt	
-do-	16th		Battalion on working parties. A football match was held in the afternoon in which the Officers drew with the NCOs of the Bn 1–1. Weather fine. G.A.S. 2/Lt	
-do-	17th		The Battalion relieved the 13th Bn E Surrey Regt in the line. Relief completed by 1.50 pm.	(3) Copy of Strength State attached

2353 Wt. W2544/1454 700,000 5/15 D. D. & L. A.D.S.S./Forms/C. 2118.

Instructions regarding War Diaries and Intelligence Summaries are contained in F. S. Regs., Part II. and the Staff Manual respectively. Title pages will be prepared in manuscript.

WAR DIARY
or
INTELLIGENCE SUMMARY.
(Erase heading not required.)

Army Form C. 2118.

Place	Date	Hour	Summary of Events and Information	Remarks and references to Appendices
	March			
In the TRENCHES	17th (Cont)		The rest of the day was quiet but about 5.0 pm the Enemy shelled Bn HQ. The weather was remarkably fine & warm & the visibility very good. [illegible] 2/Lt.	
-do-	18th		The Enemy shelled HQ getting a direct hit on the signal station with a 77mm shell. Rest of day quiet. Weather fine. Casualties nil. [illegible] 2/Lt.	
-do-	19th		Quiet day. Weather misty & cold. Casualties 1 OR killed 1 OR wounded. [illegible] 2/Lt.	
-do-	20th		Everything quiet all day. Very wet day. Casualties nil. [illegible] 2/Lt.	
-do-	21st		Day very quiet. Weather snowy. Casualties 1 OR wounded. [illegible] 2/Lt.	
-do-	22nd		Enemy got a direct hit on [illegible] setting it on fire. Owing to the prearranged scheme for such occurrences no casualties. The Company turned out [illegible] in the R. Line [illegible] MIDDLESEX LINE for the night. Rest of day quiet. Weather alternately fine & clear and overcast. Casualties 1 OR killed. 2/Lt.	
-do-	23rd		Battalion relieved by 12th [illegible] Regt. Relief completed at [illegible] 2/Lt. [illegible] Casualties nil. [illegible]	
ONTARIO CAMP	24th		Battalion training [illegible] heavy [illegible] Casualties nil. [illegible]	(4) Copy of strength state attached.

2353 Wt. W2544/1454 700,000 5/15 D. D. & L. A.D.S.S./Forms/C. 2118.

Instructions regarding War Diaries and Intelligence Summaries are contained in F. S. Regs., Part II. and the Staff Manual respectively. Title pages will be prepared in manuscript.

WAR DIARY
or
INTELLIGENCE SUMMARY.
(*Erase heading not required.*)

Army Form C. 2118.

Place	Date	Hour	Summary of Events and Information	Remarks and references to Appendices
ONTARIO CAMP	25th		Half the Battalion attended Church Parade at RENINGHELST. The remainder (200 men) attended a ~~[illegible]~~ parade at CHIPPEWA CAMP at which the Divisional Commander presented medal ribbons to such Officers NCO's & men who had not received them. The rest of the day clear. G.a.S. [illegible]	
-do-	26th		Battalion on working parties. Weather fine. 2/Lts ~~[illegible]~~ T.G.R. PACY, G.M. LITTLE, F. BRUNT, and 2/Lt A. BALLANTYNE reported for duty. G.a.S. [illegible]	
-do-	27th		The Baths at RENINGHELST were allotted to Companies. Companies training under their own arrangements when not at the Baths. A boxing competition was held in the afternoon. G.a.S. [illegible]	
-do-	28th		All platoon Commanders attended 7.0 am. parade. For the rest of the day the Battalion trained on the range and at the Brigade School. G.a.S. [illegible]	
-do-	29th		Owing to the very wet weather the Battalion did training in Camp. G.a.S. [illegible]	
-do-	30th		The Battalion relieved the 12th East Surrey Regt in the line. The Relief was completed by 1.40 pm. A new trench is being dug near NEW FARM to accommodate the Coy turned out from SUNDERLAND Ho. G.a.S. [illegible]	
In the TRENCHES	31st		Quiet day, work carried on as usual. Weather rain at intervals. Casualties. 1 O.R. wounded. G.a.S. [illegible]	(8) Copy of Strength State attached

G. McNicoll Major
Comdg. 20th. Durham L. I.

2353 Wt. W2544/1454 700,000 5/15 D. D. & L. A.D.S.S./Forms/C. 2118.

20TH (S) BN. DURHAM LIGHT INFANTRY.

(1)

STRENGTH STATE.

	OFFICERS.	O.R's.
Present with Companies.	15.	571.
Present with H.Qrs.	6.	70.
Transport Section.	1.	53.
Quartermasters Establishment.		7.
Second Army.		1.
Xth Corps H.QRS.		4.
Divisional Employ.	2.	12.
Brigade Employ.		12.
Attached to A.S.C.		4.
" L.T.Mortar Battery.		1.
" Machine Gun Coy.		2.
" Divl. Tunlg Coy.		27.
" 12th Canadian Tunlg.Coy.		9.
" 250th Tunlg. Coy.		10.
Brigade School.	1.	[illegible]
228th Field Coy.	1.	13.
Courses of Instruction.	2.	56.
Field Ambulances & D.R.S.	4.	14.
Details left with Transport.		15.
Traffic Control.		1.
Pigeon Personnel.		2.
Drainage Party.	1.	3.
Absent without leave.		1.
Attd to Camp Commandants Dept.		2.
Hutting Work.		6.
41st Divl. Base Depot.		2.
TOTAL.	33.	932.

3-5-1917. Lieut-Colonel. Comdg.

20TH (S) BN. DURHAM LIGHT INFANTRY.

STRENGTH STATE?

	OFFICERS.	O.R's.
Present in trenches with Coys.	18.	501.
Present in Trenches with H.Qrs.	6.	97.
At Transport Lines (Sick).		1[illegible].
Transport Section.	1.	54.
Quartermasters Establishment.	1.	2.
Second Army.		1.
Xth Corps H.Qrs.		[illegible].
Divisional Employ.	1.	12.
Brigade Employ.		11.
Attached to A.S.C.		4.
" L.T.Mortar Battery.		1.
" Machine Gun Coy.		5.
" Divl. Tunnelling Coy.		27.
" 250th Tunnelling Coy.		10.
" 1st Canadian Tunlg Coy.		9.
Brigade School.		8.
228th Field Coy. R.E.	1.	13.
Details left at Camp.		17.
Courses of Instruction.	2.	85.
Field Ambulances & D.R.S.	4.	54.
Traffic Control.		1.
Pigeon Personnel.		3.
Drainage Party.		2.
Under arrest at ALBERT.		1.
Attd to Camp Commandants Dept.		2.
41st Divl. Base Depot.		2.
Hutting Work.		[illegible].
Buglers remaining behind.		9.
TOTAL.	34.	945.

10-3-1917. Lieut-Colonel, Comdg.

20TH (S) BN. DURHAM LIGHT INFANTRY. (3)

STRENGTH STATE.

	OFFICERS.	O.R's.
Present in Trenches with Coys.	16.	483.
Present in Trenches with H.Qrs.	6.	91.
At Transport Lines (Sick).		10.
Transport Section.	1.	50.
Quartermasters Establishment.	1.	8.
Second Army.		1.
Xth Corps H.Qrs.		4.
Divisional Employ.	1.	11.
Brigade Employ.		13.
Attached to A.S.C.		4.
" Machine Gun Coy.		5.
" Divl. Tunnelling Coy.		27.
" 250th Tunlg. Coy.		10.
" 1st Canadian Tunlg Coy.		9.
Brigade School.		7.
228th Field Coy. R.E.	1.	12.
Attd to Flying Corps.		5.
Permanent Working Party POPERINGHE.		11.
Details left at Camp.		15.
Courses of Instruction.	4.	90.
Field Ambulances & D.R.S.	3.	37.
Traffic Control.		1.
Pigeon Personnel		3.
Drainage Party.		2.
Hutting Work. 228th Field Coy.		6.
Attd to Camp Commandants Dept.		2.
41st Divl. Base Depot.		2.
Hospital with Officer.		1.
Under Arrest at ALBERT & Escort.		4.
G.H.Q Cadet School.	1.	-
Buglers remaining behind.		16.
TOTAL.	34.	940.

17-3-1917. Lieut-Colonel. Comdg.

20th. (S) BN. DURHAM LIGHT INFANTRY. (4)

STRENGTH STATE.

	OFFICERS.	O.R's.
Present with Coys.	15.	532.
Present with H.QRS.	5.	72.
Transport Section.	1.	51.
Quartermasters Establishment.	1.	8.
Second Army.		1.
Xth Corps H.QRS.		4.
Divisional Employ.	1.	11.
Brigade Employ.	1.	14.
Attached to A.S.C.		4.
" Machine Gun Coy.		5.
" Divl. Runnelling Coy.		27.
" 250th Tunlg. Coy.		10.
" 1st Canadian Tunlg Coy.		9.
Brigade School.		7.
228th Field Coy. R.E.	1.	12.
Permanent Working Party. POPERINGHE.		10.
41st Divl. Signals.		51.
Details left at Camp.		15.
Courses of Instruction.	2.	32.
In Field Ambulances & D.R.S.	3.	35.
Traffic Control.		1.
Pigeon Personnel.		3.
Drainage Party.		2.
Leave.	1.	-
Hutting Work. 228th Field Coy.		6.
Attd to Camp Commandants Dept.		1.
41st Divl. Base Depot.		3.
Hospital with Officer.		1.
G.H.Q. Cadet School.	1½	-
TOTAL.	32.	927.

24-3-1917.

Lieut-Colonel. Comdg.

20th (S) BN. DURHAM LIGHT INFANTRY. (8)

STRENGTH STATE.

	OFFICERS.	O.R's.
Present in Trenches with Coys.	18.	508.
Present in Trenches with H.Qrs.	5.	92.
At Transport lines (Sick).		13.
Transport Section.	1.	51.
Quartermasters Establishment.	1.	8.
Second Army		1.
Xth Corps Headquarters.		4.
Divisional Employ.	1.	4.
Brigade Employ.	1.	15.
Attached to A.S.C.		4.
" L.T.Mortar Battery.		10.
" Machine Gun Coy.		5.
" Divl.Tunnelling Coy.		2.
" 1st Canadian Tunlg Coy.		9.
Brigade School.		6.
Permanent Working Party POPERINGHE.		10.
Buglers remaining behind.		10.
Divl. Training School.		6.
Armourer Sgt. at D.A.D.O.S.		1.
Details left at Camp.		16.
Courses of Instruction.	3.	40.
In Field Ambulances or D.R.S.	4.	42.
Traffic Control.		1.
Pigeon Personnel.		5.
G.H.Q.Cadet School.	1.	1.
Drainage Party.		2.
Leave.	1.	
Hutting Work. 228th Field Coy.		6.
41st Divl. Base Depot.		3.
Hospital with Officers.		2.
Attached to 237th R.E's.	1.	55.
TOTAL	37.	932.

31-3-1917.

Major, Comdg.

Instructions regarding War Diaries and Intelligence Summaries are contained in F. S. Regs., Part II. and the Staff Manual respectively. Title pages will be prepared in manuscript.

WAR DIARY
or
~~INTELLIGENCE SUMMARY.~~
(Erase heading not required.)

Army Form C. 2118.

20th Durham Light Infantry.

Vol 12

Place	Date	Hour	Summary of Events and Information	Remarks and references to Appendices
TRENCHES.	1·4·17		Quiet day, work carried on as usual. Weather, snow at intervals. Casualties 1·O·R killed 2 O·R wounded. RHL Lt	See Strength State Appendix I attached.
— do —	2·4·17		Enemy shelled MIDDLESEX LANE in the morning, and SCOTTISH WOOD all day. Weather, heavy snow falls at intervals. Casualties 1 O·R killed. RHL Lt	
— do —	3·4·17		Quiet day. At night the enemy retaliated strongly to our medium trench mortars and knocked in QUEEN VICTORIA St C.T in two places. Casualties 1 O·R killed. RHL Lt	
— do —	4·4·17		The enemy shelled our front line during the afternoon, and sent some gas shells into the R line at 7 p.m. At night the enemy again retaliated very strongly to our medium T.M's knocking in CRATER LANE C.T and the R line. Casualties 1 ~~Officer~~ 2/Lt J. A. BALLANTYNE wounded, and 1 O·R wounded. Weather fine with good visibility. RHL Lt	
— do —	5·4·17		The Battn was relieved by the 12th E. Surrey Regt, relief complete by 1.30 p.m. On return to Camp 5 Officers and 239 O·R's were inoculated. Weather, fine. Casualties nil. RHL Lt	
ONTARIO CAMP	6·4·17		The Battn, less the inoculated party who remained at Brigade School, proceeded by route march to the STEENVOORDE Area billeting the night there. Weather, beautifully fine. RHL Lt	
STEENVOORDE AREA	7·4·17		The Battn marched from the STEENVOORDE Area to the NORDPEENE Area, and billeted there. Weather, fine. RHL Lt	

A5834 Wt. W4973/M687 750,000 8/16 D. D. & L. Ltd. Forms/C.2118/13.

Instructions regarding War Diaries and Intelligence Summaries are contained in F. S. Regs., Part II. and the Staff Manual respectively. Title pages will be prepared in manuscript.

WAR DIARY
or
~~INTELLIGENCE SUMMARY.~~

(*Erase heading not required.*)

Army Form C. 2118.

20th Durham L.I.

Place	Date	Hour	Summary of Events and Information	Remarks and references to Appendices
NOORDPEENE AREA	8.4.17		The Battn marched to EPERLECQUES, and took up their new billets. Weather, fine. P.H.L. Lt. The 23rd MIDDLESEX REGT and this Battn were the only Battalions of the Brigade to complete the march without a single man falling out. P.H.L. Lt.	See Strength State Appendix II attached
EPERLECQUES	9.4.17		The day was spent in cleaning up, and inspections. The inoculated party entrained at POPERINGHE, and arrived at EPERLECQUES at 3 p.m. A lecture for all officers and N.C.O's of the Brigade was held by Lt. G.O.C. at HOULLE in the evening. He informed us that the Brigade are to make an attack on the DAMSTRASSE shortly, with this Battn in support. Weather, changeable, Snow at intervals. P.H.L. Lt. Trench map reference for DAMSTRASSE. (WYTSCHAETE. 28.SW2) O9 a.b. P.H.L. Lt.	
– do –	10.4.17		The Battn took part in Platoon training on the Battn area until 12 midday, when they returned to billets owing to the weather. The C.O lectured the Battn at 2.30 p.m. Weather, cold and windy all day. P.H.C. Lt.	
– do –	11.4.17		Platoon, and Coy training on the Battn area. The weather again interfered with training, and the Battn returned to billets at 1.30 p.m. The C.O lectured all officers at 3.30 p.m. Platoons were lectured by their officers at 6 p.m. Weather, wet all day. P.H.C. Lt.	
-do-	12.4.17		Firing on the Range, and wave attacks were practiced. Night operations at 9.30 pm when the Battn were lined up in waves not extended. Weather, Showery and cold. During the course of the mornings training firing the Lewis Gun, and rifle from the hip was carried out with great success. P.H.L. Lt.	
- do -	13.4.17		The Battn were on the Small range, and Coys practiced wave attacks on a definite objective with consolidation. The Div. Comdr seeing each Coy practicing &c. The C.O lectured the officers on return to billets at 4.30 p.m. Weather, beautifully fine all day. P.H.L.	
-do-	14.4.17		Two Companies were on the Small range in the morning practicing firing the rifle, and L.G from the hip, and throwing live bombs. Advance Guards and Outposts were practiced during the morning and afternoon, the C.O lectured the officers on return. Night operations were held at 9.30 p.m, the Battn being lined out on flags in waves. Weather, fine. P.H.L.	

A5834 Wt. W4973/M687 750,000 8/16 D. D. & L. Ltd. Forms/C.2118/13.

Army Form C. 2118.

Instructions regarding War Diaries and Intelligence Summaries are contained in F. S. Regs., Part II. and the Staff Manual respectively. Title pages will be prepared in manuscript.

WAR DIARY
or
~~INTELLIGENCE SUMMARY.~~
(Erase heading not required.)

20th Durham L.I.

Place	Date	Hour	Summary of Events and Information	Remarks and references to Appendices
EPERLECQUES.	15.4.17.		Voluntary Services were held for the Battn in the morning. A Coy defeated an R.A.M.C. Coy by 2 goals to nil in the morning. The remainder of the day was too wet for games. Weather, rainy all day. COL. NORTH returned at midday after three weeks leave. 2/Lt. W.D. CLARK and 2/Lt W.H. KIPPS reported for duty from the 3rd D.L.I. and were posted to A Coy. P.H.C.	
-do-	16.4.17		In the morning, Companies practised the attack in waves in conjunction with the other three Battalions of the Brigade. During the afternoon Coys practised lining out for digging and being held up by a strong point. Lt W.C. BROWN is appointed acting Captain whilst Commanding a Company. Weather, fine but windy. P.H.C. CAPTAIN SIM rejoined the Battn to-day, and took over the Command of C. Coy.	
-do-	17.4.17		The Battalion moved off for training but owing to the weather they were recalled to billets at 10 a.m. The remainder of the day was spent in lectures on training etc. The C.O lectured all officers at 2.30pm. Weather, wet all day. P.H.C.	
-do-	18.4.17		Owing to the bad weather the practice Attack was cancelled. Companies went in turn to the baths at HOULLE and carried out lectures, and training in billets. Weather, wet all day. P.H.C.	
-do-	19.4.17		Companies carried out the Attack with the Battalions to which they are attached. Firing on the Range, digging in, and practising Rifle Grenade Sections was carried out during the afternoon. ~~[illegible]~~ Weather, [illegible] wet.	P.H.C.
-do-	20.4.17		The Brigade practised the Attack which is to be made on the DAMSTRASSE. ~~[illegible]~~ A, B and D Companies supported respectively the 23rd Middlesex on the right, the 10th R. West Kents in the centre, and the 11th Queens on the left. C Coy provided moppers up for each Battalion. Appended is a map showing the objectives and the Brigade frontage, also the remarks made by the Army Commander (General Plumer) and the Brigadier General on the operations. P.H.C.	See Map attached Appendix III. See Remarks attached Appendix IV.

Continued

A5834 Wt. W4973/M687 750,000 8/16 D. D. & L. Ltd. Forms/C.2118/13.

Instructions regarding War Diaries and Intelligence Summaries are contained in F. S. Regs., Part II. and the Staff Manual respectively. Title pages will be prepared in manuscript.

WAR DIARY
or
INTELLIGENCE SUMMARY.
(*Erase heading not required.*)

20th Durham L.I.

Army Form C. 2118.

Place	Date	Hour	Summary of Events and Information	Remarks and references to Appendices
EPERLECQUES	Continued 20.4.17		FORMATIONS Each platoon provided 1 wave in two lines, the lines being 10 yards apart and the waves 20 yards apart. SITUATION REPORTS. A new method for sending in these reports was adopted by the Commanding Officer: Every Officer made several tracings of the Brigade front, taken from the WYTSCHAETE 28 S.W.2 map: on these maps they simply marked their own positions ~~and~~ ~~the~~ those of the enemy, and those of the troops on their right and left. The method proved most successful, and saved a great deal of unnecessary writing. ~~PHC~~ Weather, fine. P.H.C	See Strength State Appendix I attached.
– do –	21.4.17		An exact replica of the Attack which was practiced yesterday. The Corps Comdr General Morland was present. ~~Aft~~ On the way back for dinners each Battalion practiced Artillery formations, and opening out into extended order. After dinners advanced Guards were practiced. ~~PHC~~ Weather, fine.	
– do –	22.4.17		Voluntary Services were held in the morning. The Brigadier General lectured at 10.30 a.m. to the Officers & N.C.O's of the Battn. He congratulated all ranks on what had been done during the time we had been at EPERLECQUES. He expressed the hope that he would be able to see the whole Brigade together before they went into action. Weather, fine. P.H.C	
– do –	23.4.17		The Brigade, of which we formed the Vanguard marched to the NORDPEENE Area a distance of about 14 miles. We marched in threes instead of fours. The whole of this Battn were billeted in WAEMERS-CAPPEL. No men fell out on the march. Weather, fine. P.H.C	

A5834 Wt. W4973/M687 750,000 8/16 D. D. & L. Ltd. Forms/C.2118/13.

Instructions regarding War Diaries and Intelligence Summaries are contained in F. S. Regs., Part II. and the Staff Manual respectively. Title pages will be prepared in manuscript.

WAR DIARY
or
INTELLIGENCE SUMMARY.
(Erase heading not required.)

20th Durham L.I.

Army Form C. 2118.

Place	Date	Hour	Summary of Events and Information	Remarks and references to Appendices
WAEMERS-CAPPEL	24.4.17		We marched from the NORDPEENE Area to the STEENVOORDE Area, where we were billeted for the night. No men fell out. Weather, fine. P.H.C.	See Strength State Appendix VI attached
STEENVOORDE Area	25.4.17		The Battn. completed the march to RENINGHELST. A and B Coys were returned to ONTARIO CAMP, C and D Coys being housed in huts at MICMAC for a short time. Not a single man fell out on the march. We marched to-day as a Brigade. Weather fine. P.H.C.	
ONTARIO CAMP	26.4.17		The Brigadier inspected the boots of this Battn. in the morning: the remainder of the day was spent in inspections of gas helmets, box respirators, and feet. C Coy were firing on the range at CHIPPEWA. ~~The~~ Weather was fine. P.H.C. Captain CHATT reported his return, and took over the command of A Company. P.H.C.	
– do –	27.4.17		Training was carried out under Company Arrangements. All Sections were practised in the use of their own weapons. We were able to get plenty of Rifle Grenades which were distributed equally among Coys and Weather fine. P.H.C.	
– do –	28.4.17		A and B Coys were training under Company arrangements. C and D Coys are under the orders of the O.C 228th Field Coy R.E for Working Parties. Weather fine. P.H.C.	
– do –	29.4.17		The whole Battalion ~~was~~ is on working parties all day. ~~day~~ Weather, fine. ~~PHC~~ At about 3. p.m the enemy put some heavy shells near the OUDERDOM Dump and the new Railway EAST of RENINGHELST. He continued ~~doing~~ this shelling at intervals throughout the night.	
– do –	30.4.17		The Baths at RENINGHELST are allotted to the Battn to-day. C and D Coys are using the CHIPPEWA Range, the remainder are on Working Parties. Weather fine. P.H.C.	

P.W. North Lt. Col.
Cmdg 20th Durham L.I.

A5834 Wt. W4973/M687 750,000 8/16 D. D. & L. Ltd. Forms/C.2118/13.

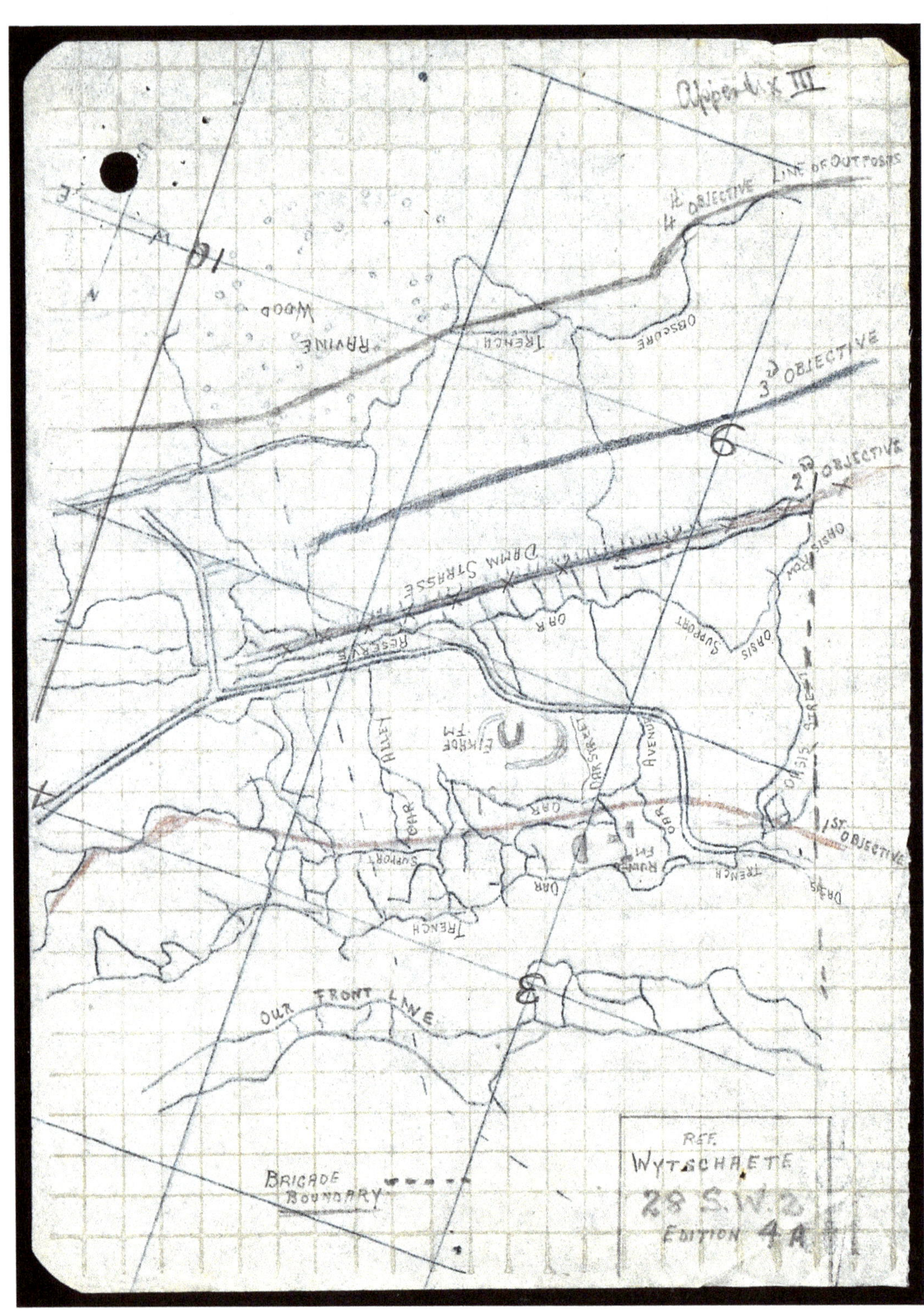

Appendix III
4th OBJECTIVE LINE OF OUTPOSTS
3rd OBJECTIVE
2nd OBJECTIVE
1ST OBJECTIVE
DAMM STRASSE
RESERVE
ALLEY
OAR
OAR STREET
AVENUE
SUPPORT
TRENCH
RUINED FM
OUR FRONT LINE
BRIGADE BOUNDARY
REF.
WYTSCHAETE
28 S.W.2
EDITION 4A

Appendix I

20TH (S) BN. DURHAM LIGHT INFANTRY.

STRENGTH STATE.

	OFFICERS.	O.R's.
Present with Companies.	17.	540.
Present with H.Qrs.	5.	70.
Transport Section.	1.	51.
QuarterMasters Establishment.	1.	8.
Second Army		1.
Xth Corps H.Qrs.		4.
Divisional Employ.	1.	4.
Brigade Employ.	1.	14.
Attd to A.S.C.		4.
" " L.T.Mortar Battery.		19.
" " Machine Gun Coy.		5.
" " Divl.Tunlg Coy.		23.
" " 1st Canadian Tunlg Coy.		9.
Brigade School.		6.
237th Field Coy. R.E.	1.	35.
Permanent Working Party POPERINGHE.		10.
Divisional Training School.		6.
Courses of Instruction.	2.	40.
In Field Ambulances and D.R.Stations.	5.	37.
Traffic Control.		1.
Pigeon Personnel.		3.
G.H.Q.Cadet School.	1.	-
Drainage Party.		2.
Leave	1.	
Hutting Work. 228th Field Coy.		6.
Base Depot.		3.
Armourer Sgt. attd to D.A.D.O.S.		1.
Hospital with Officer.		1.
Coal Guard.		7.
Escort and Prisoner at A.P.M's.		9.
TOTAL.	36.	920.

5-4-1917.

2nd Lieut.A/Adjt.
for Major, Comdg.

Appendix II.

20TH (S) BN. DURHAM LIGHT INFANTRY.

STRENGTH STATE.

	OFFICERS.	O.R's.
Present with Companies.	20.	598.
-do- H.Qrs.	4.	74.
Transport Section.	1.	53.
Quartermasters Establishment.	1.	8.
Xth Corps H.Qrs.		4.
Divisional Employ.	2.	5.
Brigade Employ.		11.
Attd. to A.S.C.		5.
" " L.T.Mortar Battery.		17.
" " Machine Gun Coy.		5.
" " Divl.Tunnlg.Coy.		22.
" " 1st Canadian Tunlg.Coy.		9.
237th Field Coy. R.E.	1.	35.
Under arrest and Escort at A.P.M's		9.
Attd to D.A.D.O.S.		1.
Hospital with Officer.		1.
Courses of Instruction.		13.
Field Ambulances & D.R.Stations.	6.	37.
Pigeon Personnel.		3.
G.H.Q.Cadet School.	1.	-
Leave.	1.	-
Base Depot.		3.
TOTAL.	37.	913.

14-4-1917.

2nd Lieut. A/Adjt.
for Major, Comdg.

Appendix IV.

Remarks by GOC Brigade (Gen Gordon)

Practice attack April 20th 1917.

1. Talking when lining up on the tapes. Absolute Silence

2. When the advance started 80% started talking & shouting. Silence must be maintained

3. The Flags are moved 40 yards from the actual objective aimed at. Lines should keep 30 yds from the flags making 70 yds in all.

4. Moppers & Runners have definite jobs to do

5. Pace should be 25 yards per minute

6. As front lines pass objectives they must halt there for a time. Never leave a line absolutely empty of men. Kill all there then move on.

7. Men when they lie out under a barrage must lie down & nothing else

8. Distance between waves too great with Middlesex very much too little with Kents & Queens.

9. Never pass with your barrage Keep 30 yds from it

After Gen Gordon had addressed the Officers and Sergeants, the Army Comdr laid special stress on the necessity for silence, and the necessity for the men to look to their Platoon Commanders who will lead them in the attack

Appendix V

20TH (S) BN. DURHAM LIGHT INFANTRY.

STRENGTH STATE.

	OFFICERS.	O.R's.
Present in Billets with Coys.	20.	594.
-do- H.QRS.	6.	76.
Transport Section.	1.	49.
Quartermasters Establishment.	1.	8.
Xth Corps H.Qrs.		4.
Divisional Employ.	2.	5.
Brigade Employ.		21.
Attd. to A.S.C.		5.
" " L.T.M.Battery.		17.
" " M.G.Coy.		6.
" " Divl.Tunlg Coy.		22.
Courses of Instruction.		1.
Field Ambulances & DR.Stations.	8.	28.
Pigeon Personnel.		3.
237th Field Coy. R.E.	1.	34.
5th Army Wireless Coy.		1.
1st Canadian Tunlg Coy.		9.
Hospital with Officer.		1.
Attd to D.A.D.O.S.		1.
Under arrest & Escort at A.P.M's.		9.
Base Depot.		1.
TOTAL.	39.	895.

21-4-1917.

2nd Lieut.A/Adjt.
for Lieut-Colonel. Comdg.

Appendix VI

20TH (S) BN. DURHAM LIGHT INFANTRY.

STRENGTH STATE.

	OFFICERS.	O.R's.
Present in Billets with Coys.	21.	453.
-do- H.Qrs.	6.	70.
Transport Section.	1.	47.
Quartermasters Establishment.	1.	14.
Xth Corps H.Qrs.		4.
Divisional Employ.	2.	7.
Brigade Employ.		20.
Attd to A.S.C.		5.
" " L.T.M.Battery.		15.
" " Divl. Tunlg.Coy.		23.
" " 1st Canadian Tunlg Coy.		59.
Brigade School.		1.
237th Field Coy. R.E.	1.	33.
Attd to D.A.D.O.S.		1.
Courses of Instruction.	2.	7.
Field Ambulances & D.R.Stations.	1.	19.
Traffic Control.		1.
Pigeon Personnel.		3.
Leave (Sick).	2.	-
Hutting work. 233rd Field Coy.		6.
Musketry Course.		55.
Course at Brigade School.	1.	46.
Divisional Guard.		8.
TOTAL.	38.	897.

28-4-1917.

2nd Lieut A/Adjt.
for Lieut-Colonel.Comdg

Confidential

WAR DIARY

20th (S) Bn. of Durham Light Infantry

from 1st May 1917 — 31st May 1917.

Vol 13

Army Form C. 2118

WAR DIARY
or
INTELLIGENCE SUMMARY
(Erase heading not required.)

20th Durham L.I.

Instructions regarding War Diaries and Intelligence Summaries are contained in F. S. Regs., Part II. and the Staff Manual respectively. Title Pages will be prepared in manuscript.

Place	Date	Hour	Summary of Events and Information	Remarks and references to Appendices
ONTARIO CAMP	1.5.17		A and B Coys carried out training under Company arrangements. C and D being on working parties as usual. All men had baths to-day. Weather fine. P.H.C. [illegible]	
— do —	2.5.17		A and B trained under their own arrangements. C & D were on working parties. At about 10.10 pm the Gas alarm sounded whereupon all men stood to for half an hour until orders were issued that normal conditions were to be resumed. At 1.20 am there was a fire alarm. The Commanding Officer's hut and the Orderly Room were burnt to the ground. All official papers and documents & most of the Commanding Officer's kit were burnt. As the huts were of tar, all efforts to put out the flames proved fruitless. Weather fine. P.H.C. [illegible]	
MICMAC CAMP	3.5.17		The Battalion relieved the 21st K.R.R. Regiment to-day. Relief was complete by 9.30 am. C and D Coys went to DICKEBUSCH & A & B to MICMAC. The Battn is in Reserve & will be on on working parties. Casualties 2/Lt LITTLE G.M. wounded. 1 O.R. wounded. Weather, fine. PHC [illegible]	
— do —	4.5.17		All four Companies are finding working parties while we are in Reserve. All available Officers did a tactical scheme in the morning. Our heavy artillery was very busy during the night. Casualties, nil. Weather, fine. PHC [illegible]	
— do —	5.5.17		The Commanding Officer lectured all officers & N.C.O's at 5.15 pm. At night the heavy artillery of both sides was very active. The enemy's 8 inch Naval gun (probably) shelled the new railway intermittently. Casualties nil. Weather fine. P.H.C. [illegible]	1. Copy of Strength State attached
— do —	6.5.17.		There were Voluntary Services for all denominations. The enemy got two direct hits on the D Company officers' dugout in DICKEBUSCH during the night, luckily none was hurt. Casualties, 4 O.R's wounded. Weather, fine. PHC [illegible]	
— do —	7.5.17		During the night of the 6th/7th the enemy heavily shelled our back areas. The men of C & D Coys in DICKEBUSCH were forced to spend most of the night in the fields. Throughout the day the shelling continued. At 8.55 pm every gun on the 2nd Army front fired at intense rates for 5 minutes on the enemy's communications, this, with a view to stopping the shelling of our back areas at night. It was an unforgettable sight as the whole of the YPRES salient seemed one flame. The enemy retaliated about 10 pm, so at 11 pm the five minutes burst was repeated, again at 11.15 pm, for the remainder of the night the enemy was fairly quiet. Casualties nil. Weather fine. PHC. [illegible]	

1875 Wt. W593/826 1,000,000 4/15 J.B.C. & A. A.D.S.S./Forms/C. 2118.

Army Form C. 2118.

Instructions regarding War Diaries and Intelligence Summaries are contained in F. S. Regs., Part II. and the Staff Manual respectively. Title Pages will be prepared in manuscript.

WAR DIARY
or
INTELLIGENCE SUMMARY
(Erase heading not required.)

20th Durham L.I.

Place	Date	Hour	Summary of Events and Information	Remarks and references to Appendices
MICMAC CAMP	8.5.17.		A very quiet day. DICKEBUSCH was not shelled as heavily as usual, & the men were not disturbed at night. Casualties nil, Weather fine.	Ref. WYTSCHAETE 28.S.W.Ed.5a.
– do –	9.5.17.		There were the ordinary working parties. At about 9.15 p.m. several red lights went up from the Hill 60 Sector, to the right of P & O communication trench. The retaliation of our guns was prompt, & the firing continued for 3/4 hour. The enemy had apparently intended to make a raid, but was stopped by our artillery. Casualties, 1 O.R. wounded, weather fine. P.H.C.	
– do –	10.5.17.		A quiet day. The Commanding Officer gave some officers lessons in riding & jumping in the evening. Weather fine. P.H.C.	
– do –	11.5.17.		The Batt.n moved to-day. D Coy went to G.H.Q. Advanced 2nd Line, A and B Coys & H.Q. to DICKEBUSCH Lake, C Coy remained at MICMAC. Working parties as usual. Casualties nil, weather fine. P.H.C.	2. {Copy of Strength State attached}
TRENCHES	12.5.17.		We relieved the 23rd MIDDLESEX REGT in the line in our old Sector to-day. Relief complete by 5.15 pm. At 9.15 pm the enemy put a few 15.0 c.m shells in the vicinity of the BRASSERIE. During the evening our heavies fired on NORTH REDOUBT. Casualties nil, Weather fine. P.H.C. Draft of 18 O.R. trained reported their arrival. P.H.C.	DRAFTS from 3rd D.L.I.
– do –	13.5.17.		The enemies Artillery was only active on back areas notably LANKHOF FARM. Our Art. were very busy all day, fire being directed chiefly on points round the DAMSTRASSE. Wire was cut for 1/4 hour with very little retaliation. Casualties, 2 O.R. wounded. Weather fine. Draft of 52 O.R. reported their arrival. P.H.C.	
– do –	14.5.17.		Our Art. was very active all day wire cutting, & firing on front, support, & R lines. Except for a short burst from 4–4.30 pm when the shelled BOIS CONFLUENT & the R line, the enemy was only carrying out counter battery work. Casualties 1 O.R. wounded. Weather fine. Draft of 46 O.R. reported their arrival. P.H.C.	P.H.C. Lieut.
– do –	15.5.17.		Our Art. were again very active all day carrying out the preliminary bombardments according to programme, much damage was done to the enemies wire & trenches by our M.T.M's & 18 pounders at 6–6.30 pm. The enemy Art were more active, counter battery work in the early morning & at 1.30 pm they shelled our right sector at top of P & O with 7.7's & 10.5's. At 6.30 pm he replied to our T.M strafe, & knocked in our front line in two places. With a view to finding out whether the enemy was holding his front line, two patrols went out at 10.30 p.m, & found that his front line is still held, the wire being very weak. Casualties 2/Lt. JENNINGS and 1 O.R. wounded. Weather fine. P.H.C.	
– do –	16.5.17.		Enemy shelled our front, support & R lines, intermittently during the morning. At 2 pm till 6 pm our Artillery carried on their bombardment of the enemy front & support lines, much damage was done. Another T.M strafe at 7.30 pm has wiped out practically all the enemy wire opposite our front. Casualties nil. Weather, Showery with bad visibility. P.H.C.	

1875 Wt. W593/826 1,000,000 4/15 J.B.C. & A. A.D.S.S./Forms/C. 2118.

Instructions regarding War Diaries and Intelligence Summaries are contained in F. S. Regs., Part II. and the Staff Manual respectively. Title Pages will be prepared in manuscript.

WAR DIARY
or
~~INTELLIGENCE SUMMARY~~

(*Erase heading not required.*)

20th Durham L.I.

Army Form C. 2118.

Place	Date	Hour	Summary of Events and Information	Remarks and references to Appendices
TRENCHES	17.5.17		Our bombardment continued most of the day though the light was poor. The enemy art was also fairly active especially on our S & R lines. At 8.30 pm the enemy strafed S.14 & the S line for 20 minutes doing considerable damage, but without causing casualties, this was with minnies & 10.5 cm's. At night we carried out a silent raid with the object of taking a prisoner. See attached report with operation order. Casualties Nil. Weather dull. PHC	
-do-	18.5.17		The enemy shelled front, support, & R lines in retaliation for our continuous bombardment which was aided by better visibility. Our raiders again attempted to take a prisoner at night but the enemy were waiting for them, & after suffering 2 casualties our part, withdrew. The Batt on our right S. Lancs attempted to enter enemy trenches later on, & fared very badly the enemy was obviously prepared for them. Casualties 2 O.R wounded. Weather fine	
-do- & Micmac	19.5.17		The Batt was relieved by the 12th E. Surrey Regt, relief being complete by 11.30 am. We are now in Camp at MICMAC in Reserve finding Working parties. Casualties, Nil. Weather fine. PHC	App 3. Copy of Strength State attached.
Micmac camp	20.5.17		All companies were on working parties and training was carried out under company arrangements when possible. Casualties. OR Three casualties occurred to men on working parties. Weather fine. 2/Lt W.G. PENRICE & 2/Lt A.G. RODEN reported for Duty, from the 3rd D.L.I.	
-do-	21.5.17		All companies were on working parties, D Coy were allotted the baths at Chippewa. A change of clothing was obtained. Training was carried out where possible. Casualties Nil. Weather fine.	
-do-	22.5.17		All companies were on working parties. Coy training was carried out at Brigade School for a short period. All Officers & NCOs visited Model of trenches at Reninghelst. Casualties Nil. Weather fine.	
-do-	23.5.17		All companies were on working parties & remainder in camp carried out training under Coy arrangements. Casualties Nil. Weather fine	
-do-	24.5.17		All companies were on working parties & the range at Chippewa was allotted to Companies. Training under Coy arrangements was carried out where possible. Casualties O.R. 1 wounded. Weather fine.	

1875 Wt. W593/826 1,000,000 4/15 J.B.C. & A. A.D.S.S./Forms/C. 2118.

Instructions regarding War Diaries and Intelligence Summaries are contained in F. S. Regs., Part II. and the Staff Manual respectively. Title Pages will be prepared in manuscript.

WAR DIARY
or
INTELLIGENCE SUMMARY
(Erase heading not required.)

Army Form C. [illegible]8

Place	Date	Hour	Summary of Events and Information	Remarks and references to Appendices
MicMac Camp.	25:5:17		All companies were on working parties. Any men remaining in Camp carried out training under Coy arrangement. Wounded O.R. 1. Weather fine. [initials]	
-do-	26:5:17		All companies were on working parties. There were no casualties. Weather fine. [initials]	1. Copy of Strength State attached.
-do-	27:5:17		All companies were on working parties. There were voluntary Church services. Casualties Nil. Weather fine. [initials]	
-do-	28:5:17		All companies were on working parties. Two Companies were inspected by the M.O. Casualties Wounded O.R. 1. Weather fine. [initials]	
-do-	29:5:17		All companies were on working parties. Two Companies were inspected by the M.O. Casualties O.R. Wounded 3. Weather fine. [initials]	
-do-	30:5:17		All companies were on working parties. Any men available were trained under Coy arrangements. Casualties. Wounded O.R. 1. Weather fine. [initials]	
-do-	~~31:5:17~~		All ~~companies were on working parties. Any men available were trained under Coy arrangements.~~ Casualties Nil. Weather fine. [initials]	
do	30:5:17		An attempt was made to raid enemy line near N. Redoubt with assistance of Artillery. There was a bright moon & a still night. Arrangement was for supporting party to get near enemy front and send for Raiders and when raiders reached them signal for Artillery to open on enemy front & support lines. Signals to be sent by telephone taken out into NO MANS Land. This they did & then rushed the enemy's front line trench when Artillery lifted on to support lines. Enemy bolted but left no wounded or prisoners in the trench. Our casualties were 2 men slightly wounded. [initials]	
-do-	31:5:17		All coys were on working parties.	

P. W. North[illegible] Lt Col.
Commanding 20th Durham Light Infantry

1875 Wt. W593/826 1,000,000 4/15 J.B.C. & A. A.D.S.S./Forms/C. 2118.

20th (S) Bn Durham Light Infantry.

DAILY STATE.

	Officers	O. R's.
Present with Coys.	18	402
" " H/Qrs.	6	67
Transport	1	48
Q.M's Establishment	1	17
Second Army	.	7
Xth Corps H.Qrs.		2
Divisional Employ	2	8
Brigade "		19
attd to A.S.C.		5
" " L.T. Mortar Battery		14
" " Divl Tunnelling Coy.		24
23rd Field Coy. R.E.	1	33
228th " " "		10
Brigade School		2
" " (Course of Instn)	1	40
Field Ambulances & D.R. Station.	1	23
Courses of Instruction	1	36
Pigeon personnel.	4	3
Traffic Control		1
attd to D.A.D.O.S.		1
Divisional Guard.		8
Sick Leave.	2	–
Musketry Course.		54
Escort & Prisoner at A.P.M's.		4
Hutting Work.		8
1st Canadian Tunnelling Coy.		59
	37	895

5-5-17.

2nd Lt. A/Adjt.
for Lt.-Col. Comdg.

20th (S) Bn Durham L. I.

(2)

DAILY STATE

	Officers	O.R.s
Present with Coys.	15	392
" " H.Qrs.	5	64
Transport	1	47
Qr Mrs Establishment	2	24
Second Army		7
Xth Corps H.Qrs.		2
Divisional Employ	1	8
Brigade "		20
		5
Attd to A.S.C.		15
" " L.T.M. Battery		24
" " Divl. Tunlg Coy.		59
" " 1st Canadian Tunlg Coy.		
233rd Field Coy R.E.	1	33
Brigade Schools		2
" " (Course of Instr)	1	40
Field Ambulance & D.R.Station	1	38
Courses of Instruction	8	42
Pigeon Personnel		3
Traffic Control		4
Attd to D.A.D.O.S.		1
Leave	2	1
Musketry Course		51
Hutting Work		8
Ambleteuse Rest Camp	1	12
Hospital with Officers		1
	39	903

12-5-17

Capt. a/Adjt
for Lt Col. Comdg.

20th (S) Bn. Durham L.I.

DAILY STATE

(3)

	Officers	O.R's
Present with Coys	13	541
" " HQrs.	6	71
Transport Section	1	49
Qr. Mr. Estab.	1	21
2nd Army		7
X rd Corps H.Qrs.		2
Divisional Employ	2	8
Brigade "	1	20
Attd to A.S.C.		5
" " L.T.M. Battery.		16
" " Divl Tunly Coy.		24
" " 1st Canadian Tunly Coy.		59
233rd Field Coy. R.E.	1	33
Brigade School		2
Field Ambulance & D.R. Stations	1	36
Courses of Instruction.	9	40
Musketry Course,		23
Pigeon Personnel.		2
D.A.D.O.S.		1
Traffic Control.		4
Hutting Work		8
Leave	1	1
Rest Camp	1	12
Hospital with Officers		2
Trade Test.		2
	37	989

[signature]

19-5-17

Capt. a/adjt.
for Lt. Col. Comdg.

20th (S) Bn. Durham L.I.

(4)

DAILY STATE

	Officers	O.R.'s
Present with Coys.	16	502
" " H.Qrs.	5	64
Transport Lines	1	49
Qr. Mr. Establishment.	1	17
Second Army.		7
Xth Corps H.Qrs.		2
Divisional Employ.	2	7
Bde "	1	21
Attd to A.S.C.		5
" " L.T.M. Battery.		24
" " Machine Gun Coy.		18
" " Divisional Tunlg Coy.		24
Brigade School.		5
Courses of Instruction.	6	26
Field Ambulances & D.R. Stations.	2	28
Traffic Control.		4
Pigeon Personnel		3
On leave.	2	3
233rd Field Coy. R.E.	1	31
1st Canadian Tunlg Coy.		58
Hutting Work.		8
Rest Camp		5
Musketry Course.		23
D.A.D.O.S.		1
Trade Test		2
Hospital with Officer.		1
41st Divl. Baths.		2
Brigade School (Course)	3	39
	40	979

26-5-17.

J. Chapman [signature]

2nd Lt. Adjt.
for Lt-Col. Comdg.

20th D. L. I.

WAR DIARY
or
INTELLIGENCE SUMMARY.
(Erase heading not required.)

Instructions regarding War Diaries and Intelligence Summaries are contained in F. S. Regs., Part II. and the Staff Manual respectively. Title pages will be prepared in manuscript.

Army Form C. 2118.

123/41

Vol 14

Place	Date	Hour	Summary of Events and Information	Remarks and references to Appendices
Lugwerp Camp	1.6.17		The 20th D.L.I. was relieved at 2 am by the 26th Batt. of the Royal Fusiliers. The relieving Batt. took over the working parties from 3 pm of the 1.6.17. The Batt. proceeded to Woodcote Camp. At 5.0 [illegible] [illegible] [illegible] were carried out under company arrangements. Casualties 3 OR wounded. Weather fine, visibility, [illegible]	
Woodcote Camp	2.6.17		All companies training under Coy arrangements up to midday. After midday the N.C.Os and men took part in a Boxing competition and attended Divisional Horse Show at Reninghelst. Casualties O.R. Killed 6 [illegible] 239 Field Coy R.E.	[illegible]
"	3.6.17		Church parades and inspections under Coy arrangements. Lecture at 2 PM to all officers and NCOs by 2nd Lt. [illegible] on the Lewis gun. B and D Coys visited Baths for change of clothing. Casualties nil. Weather fine.	[illegible]
"	4.6.17		Part of Batt. on working parties [illegible] remainder carried out training under Coy arrangements at 10 am. The [illegible] General spoke to the men in camp at conclusion of which the Batt. gave [illegible] cheers. During the afternoon the officers had riding lessons. Casualties nil. Weather [illegible]	[illegible]
"	5.6.17		The Batt. had the morning and afternoon as a holiday. Batt. sports were arranged and carried out, all Coys being well represented in all the events. Prizes were given at the end of sports. At 6.30 pm the Batt. [illegible] Woodcote Camp for the G.H.Q. 2nd Line from [illegible] [illegible] the remainder of the Batt. moving off by Platoons at intervals to the G.H.Q. 2nd Line. Casualties 1 accidentally wounded. Weather fine, visibility good.	
Trenches G.H.Q. 2nd Line	6.6.17		Several of our aeroplanes were over the enemy lines flying low at daybreak and there was considerable aerial activity throughout the day on our part. No German aeroplanes could be sighted. The enemy shelled Ridgewood and Scottish wood neighbourhood with 4.2 and 5.9 and shrapnel. The Batt. rested during the day and spent a quiet time. At 12 midnight the Batt. moved off by Companies at 5 minute intervals to the assembly area, where tapes were laid out for the Batt. to form up on. ~~The [illegible]~~ The night was fine and fairly light, weather fine. Casualties 2 killed, 2 wounded.	Copied from 2nd Bn

A6945 Wt. W11422/M1160 350,000 12/16 D. D. & L. Forms/C./2118/14.

Instructions regarding War Diaries and Intelligence Summaries are contained in F. S. Regs., Part II. and the Staff Manual respectively. Title pages will be prepared in manuscript.

WAR DIARY
or
INTELLIGENCE SUMMARY.
(Erase heading not required.)

Army Form C. 2118.

Place	Date	Hour	Summary of Events and Information	Remarks and references to Appendices
near St Eloi	7.6.17		The Battn formed up on the Tapes and were in position at 2AM Orders had previously been received concerning the attacks in which we were to take part in today. This was to be a large offensive movement and we were to be in support forming the 7th and 8th waves. According to [illegible] front of 600 or [illegible]. Three companies were detailed to form the 7th and 8th waves and the remaining company was distributed by half platoons throughout the Bde front to act as moppers up. Zero hour was 3.10 AM. At Zero the mine near St Eloi went up and at Zero + 3 the Bn moved forward and [illegible] without stopping to its objective. All the objectives were taken. Our losses were not heavy, this was due to the fact that the whole Battn pushed forward without a stop to the enemy front and support lines, the enemy barrage fell [illegible] behind [us?] and had we NOT been well closed up and moved [quickly?] our casualties would have been considerably heavier. On arrival at the objectives the moppers up (consisting of 50% of [illegible]) of the Bn. soon cleared the line. A large number of enemy dead were found in the front and support lines – killed by our own artillery barrage. Meanwhile the remainder of the	

A6945 Wt. W11422/M1160 350,000 12/16 D. D. & L. Forms/C./2118/14.

[illegible]

Instructions regarding War Diaries and Intelligence Summaries are contained in F. S. Regs., Part II. and the Staff Manual respectively. Title pages will be prepared in manuscript.

Army Form C. 2118.

WAR DIARY
or
INTELLIGENCE SUMMARY.
(*Erase heading not required.*)

Place	Date	Hour	Summary of Events and Information	Remarks and references to Appendices
Near St Eloi	7.6.17		Battn pushed forward and succeeded in digging a good strong line of trenches, strong points &c.	Appendix I
			Special attention was given to the traverses, these being made about 14 ft across as enfilading	A list
			fire was expected and afterwards received from our left flank. Our trenches were dug well in	of captured
			front of the existing lines which proved very successful as the enemy shelled continually hitting	war material
			chiefly their old line, therefore doing little damage. The line of machine gun positions were chosen	is attached
			in front of our leading line of trenches. They had excellent positions, the field of fire and cover	Appendix II
			from view being especially good. As soon as moppers up had finished their work they joined	~~[illegible]~~
			the diggers & salvage parties so as to get things in order as soon as possible, to await	~~[illegible]~~
			& prepare for a counter attack. No souvenir hunting was allowed, therefore no time was lost.	Operation
			Our heavies & also the German heavies were extremely active throughout the day & night. The	Order attached
			morale of the Battn was exceptionally good and was very excellent. It was different from the German	
			Morale, as the Enemy seemed to be shaken to breaking point. The 35th Division was opposed	
			to us, and they were chiefly Prussians, Bavarians & Poles. One captured officer stated "We are done	
			the English are too good for us" Throughout the operation dispositions were rendered on Maps	
			and the system worked excellently. All unwounded prisoners were used to assist us with our	
			wounded, and to carry stores, water &c. We recd congratulatory letters from Bde, Division, Corps, Army & GOC.	[illegible]
			Casualties 2/Lt UPTON and 2/Lt PENRICE killed. 2/Lt KIPPS wounded. OR killed 8, 85 wounded 7 missing 2 gassed	
			Our aeroplanes were extremely active & Artillery & Machine Gun barrages very good. Weather fine visibility good	

A6945 Wt. W11422/M1160 350,000 12/16 D. D. & L. Forms/C./2118/14.

Instructions regarding War Diaries and Intelligence Summaries are contained in F. S. Regs., Part II. and the Staff Manual respectively. Title pages will be prepared in manuscript.

WAR DIARY
or
INTELLIGENCE SUMMARY.
(Erase heading not required.)

Army Form C. 2118.

Place	Date	Hour	Summary of Events and Information	Remarks and references to Appendices
Near St Eloi	8.6.17		The Battn carried out consolidation operations paying especial attention to the traverses making them 12ft to 14ft across, as enfilading fire from 5.9's & shrapnel were being sent over from the left flank by the Germans. Salving Operations were continued and dumps were added to. A fairly quiet day was spent. During the night about 7.30 pm one of our aeroplanes dropped the signal that the enemy were preparing for a counter attack. At that time the enemy put over a strong barrage using guns of all calibres. Our guns opened out immediately and for an hour and a half all the guns were firing. Spasmodic firing continued throughout the night and the machine guns were busy sweeping the German lines. Information from prisoners proves that machine gun fire is extremely unpleasant for the enemy, causing them to have many casualties and rendering it difficult for parties of enemy to walk & carry ammunition rations &c, thus playing havoc with their morale. Our artillery and enemy artillery and M.Gs active. Fifteen (15) of our machines could be counted up at once and the aerial work was active throughout the day. Our observation balloons were all up, whereas very few German Balloons could be seen & their aeroplanes were very inconspicuous. A strong line of wire now in position.	
			Weather fine Visibility good	
			Casualties 6 O.R. killed & wounded.	[initials]

A6945 Wt. W11422/M1160 350,000 12/16 D. D. & L. Forms/C./2118/14.

Instructions regarding War Diaries and Intelligence Summaries are contained in F. S. Regs., Part II. and the Staff Manual respectively. Title pages will be prepared in manuscript.

WAR DIARY
or
INTELLIGENCE SUMMARY.
(*Erase heading not required.*)

Army Form C. 2118.

Place	Date	Hour	Summary of Events and Information	Remarks and references to Appendices
Near St Eloi	9.6.17		Consolidating & salvage operation was carried out. Much sand bagging done as soil was very light and sandy. Artillery both ours and enemy's continued firing spasmodically throughout the day livening up a little as night came, heavies chiefly being used. The enemy sent over 5.9's, 4.2's, whizz bangs & shrapnel. We had few casualties being well protected in deep narrow trenches. Our aeroplanes were active and two German aeroplanes came over our lines at 6.30 pm flying however at a great height. Weather fine visibility good.	
			Casualties 2 O R died of wounds 4 wounded.	WJ [illegible]
Near St Eloi	10.6.17		At early morning it was misty and cool. Visibility at first was bad. Two German aeroplanes flew over our front line at 6.50 A.M. They were immediately driven back by our Lewis Gun Fire. The Battn carried out consolidating & salvage operations. A quiet day was spent. At 10.30 pm our Red lights went up in front of us. This was the signal for the Artillery to put up a barrage, as an enemy attack was expected. The artillery & machine guns immediately opened out a terrific fire putting a good barrage up. Before long the German guns of all callibres opened out, and German S.O.S. Rockets and lights could be seen. They evidently at this point were expecting an attack from us. Violent artillery and machine gun fire was continued until 11.30 pm, at which time the rate of fire slackened	

A6945 Wt. W11422/M1160 350,000 12/16 D. D. & L. Forms/C./2118/14.

Army Form C. 2118.

Instructions regarding War Diaries and Intelligence Summaries are contained in F. S. Regs., Part II. and the Staff Manual respectively. Title pages will be prepared in manuscript.

WAR DIARY
or
INTELLIGENCE SUMMARY.
(Erase heading not required.)

Place	Date	Hour	Summary of Events and Information	Remarks and references to Appendices
			Contd	
Near St Eloi	10:6:17		Our guns throughout the night kept up spasmodic firing on his front & back areas and the Germans did likewise, heavies chiefly being used. (5.9's, 4.2's & shrapnel) Little damage was done where our Battn was, although the trenches were knocked in in several places, receiving direct hits. Both ours & enemy aeroplanes were active throughout the day. Weather. Misty early morning fine later. Casualties 3 O.R's Wounded.	[illegible]
Near St. Eloi	11:6:17		Work comprised chiefly sandbagging and revetting of trenches. A quiet day was spent very few shells being sent over by enemy. Our observation balloons were well up & the aerial work was active. A & B Coys were relieved at 6pm C & D Coys remaining. A & B Coys went to the R. line situate near the Bois Confluent. A quiet night was spent. Weather. In the morning inclined to be showery later fine. Casualties 7 OR's Wounded	[illegible]
Near St Eloi	12:6:17		At daybreak several enemy aeroplanes & two enemy observation balloons were up. We had about a dozen observation balloons up and our aeroplanes were active throughout the day. Throughout the day heavy artillery both ours and the German's firing all day. At 6pm C & D Coys were relieved & joined the remainder of the Battn in the R line near Bois Confluent. A & B Coys were in	

A6945 Wt. W11422/M1160 350,000 12/16 D. D. & L. Forms/C./2118/14.

Instructions regarding War Diaries and Intelligence Summaries are contained in F. S. Regs., Part II, and the Staff Manual respectively. Title pages will be prepared in manuscript.

Army Form C. 2118.

WAR DIARY
or
INTELLIGENCE SUMMARY.
(Erase heading not required.)

Place	Date	Hour	Summary of Events and Information	Remarks and references to Appendices
			Contd	
R. Line (Near Bois Confluent)	12.6.17		the R line itself & C & D Coys were just behind in Bivouacs. A quiet night spent.	
			Weather fine visibility good	
			Casualties Nil	
R Line	13.6.17		The Battn paraded under Coy arrangements. Rapid loading & firing & giving of targets being especially noted. Inspections were held, and a programme of work followed.	
			There was great aerial activity on both sides and several duels were fought in the air.	
			Weather fine. Casualties Nil	
R. Line	14.6.17		The Battn spent a quiet day up till mid-day. Orders had been received that the 20th D.L.I. were to be in support to the 122nd INFANTRY Bde. who were taking	[illegible]
			Zero hour to be 7.30 pm. The 122nd INFANTRY BRIGADE were successful and the Battn returned to the R LINE BIVOUACS, the 20th D.L.I. not being called upon to take any further part. At 7.30 pm the enemy sent over 4.2's and 5.9's, and shrapnel and a considerable quantity of shells fell near where we were, without doing any damage. The weather was fine with visibility good.	
			Casualties 2 OR's wounded	

A6945 Wt. W11422/M1160 350,000 12/16 D. D. & L. Forms/C./2118/14.

Army Form C. 2118.

Instructions regarding War Diaries and Intelligence Summaries are contained in F. S. Regs., Part II. and the Staff Manual respectively. Title pages will be prepared in manuscript.

WAR DIARY
or
INTELLIGENCE SUMMARY.
(Erase heading not required.)

Place	Date	Hour	Summary of Events and Information	Remarks and references to Appendices
Old R. Line (near Bois Confluent)	15.6.17		The Battn paraded under Company arrangements. Special attention being paid to Musketry. Lieut Hand started a musketry class and three N.C.O's per Company to attend. Range cards and judging distances were taken, and lectures were given. Weather fine. There was much aerial activity on both sides. A quiet day was spent. Casualties Nil. [initials]	Appendix III Strength State attached
Old R. Line	16.6.17		The Companies carried out their programmes under their own arrangements. programmes of work being sent into the Orderly Room to be approved of by the C.O. The guns were quiet. Aerial activity during the day on both sides, several Boche planes coming well over our lines. Weather fine, visibility good. Special Musketry Class held for N.C.O's. Casualties 3 O.R's wounded [initials]	
Old R. Line	17.6.17		Work carried out under Company arrangements. The Special Musketry class was held. The guns were quiet. Aerial activity Normal. Weather fine. The new line of trenches to be taken over by the Battn was reconnoitred during the evening. Casualties Nil. [initials]	

A6945 Wt. W11422/M1160 350,000 12/16 D. D. & L. Forms/C./2118/14.

Instructions regarding War Diaries and Intelligence Summaries are contained in F. S. Regs., Part II. and the Staff Manual respectively. Title pages will be prepared in manuscript.

WAR DIARY
or
INTELLIGENCE SUMMARY.
(Erase heading not required.)

Army Form C. 2118.

Place	Date	Hour	Summary of Events and Information	Remarks and references to Appendices
Old R line	18.6.17		Work was carried out during the morning and afternoon under company arrangements. The N.C.O. musketry class was continued. ~~During~~ 16 men per company received a quarter of an hours instruction in the German maxim gun. ~~The~~ The afternoon was thundery, and rain fell at intervals ~~during~~ until the morning of the 19.6.17. Officers commanding companies went up during the evening to reconnoitre the new sector to be taken over by the Batt. 2nd Lieut SHEPHERDSON with Batt. Hdqrs went up at 7.30 pm to establish a new Batt. Hdq at O 4 b 25:45. Aerial activity normal. 12 German Balloons were counted early in the morning. On the approach of the rain all Balloons came down. Casualties nil	
			[illegible] 2Lt.	
Old R. line	19.6.17		At 3 AM one officer per coy with one NCO per platoon went up to take ~~up~~ over the new line of trenches to be held by the Batt. OPTIC trench from O 11 a 9½ 9½ to its junction with OBLIQUE ROW and OBLIQUE ROW. They remained up all day till dusk, when they with guides from 12 E SURREY REGT	

Instructions regarding War Diaries and Intelligence Summaries are contained in F. S. Regs., Part II. and the Staff Manual respectively. Title pages will be prepared in manuscript.

WAR DIARY
or
INTELLIGENCE SUMMARY.
(Erase heading not required.)

Army Form C. 2118.

Place	Date	Hour	Summary of Events and Information	Remarks and references to Appendices
O4 A	22.6.17		at 3 AM. Two enemy apparently lost were seen standing in front of wood opposite the strongpoint. Several rifles fired upon them one was believed hit and staggered into the wood the other followed. Our artillery [illegible] find targets for retaliation few and unsatisfactory. The observation being bad, consequently the retaliation seems somewhat ineffective. Trenches still very muddy. [illegible] casualties 3 OR'S killed × [illegible]	× Major G. McNICHOLL D.S.O wounded
O4 A	23.6.17		Enemy artillery active against our lines during the early morning and [illegible] at intervals afterwards. Our artillery twice barraged OBLIQUE trench. No lights shown. At night the Batt. was relieved by the 10 R W Kents and went into support. H.Q being at Spoil Bank and the companies stopping in the old German front line. Three of the companies were relieved at once each using a different route. This greatly hastened the proceedings, where delay might have been the cause of many casualties. The [illegible] behind White CHATEAU was bridged by Capt Anson 228th Coy RE by 9 30 PM, thus making the right-hand route practicable. Casualties 3 OR'S killed 3 OR'S wounded [illegible]	17 OR'S wounded Appendix Strength State attached

A6945 Wt. W11422/M1160 350,000 12/16 D. D. & L. Forms/C./2118/14.

Instructions regarding War Diaries and Intelligence Summaries are contained in F. S. Regs., Part II, and the Staff Manual respectively. Title pages will be prepared in manuscript.

WAR DIARY
or
INTELLIGENCE SUMMARY.
(Erase heading not required.)

Army Form C. 2118.

Place	Date	Hour	Summary of Events and Information	Remarks and references to Appendices
Spoil Bank	24.6.17.		The Battn had no work during the day except for C Coy who as carrying company carried meals and water up to the R.W.Kents and their night rations. The other 3 companies wired the Blue line at night. The day was fine throughout. Casualties 1 OR killed 5 ORs wounded. [illegible] 2nd Lt	
Spoil Bank	25.6.17		Work was carried on as for the 24th but carrying parties by day were cancelled. There was some intermittent shelling near the trenches occupied by the Battn which started on the 24th. Casualties 1 OR killed 4 wounded. [illegible] 2nd Lt Copied from 2nd Lt F Bourne	
Spoil Bank.	26.6.17		There was more rain during the night. Work was as for the 25th with the addition of a carrying party at night for the 1st Canadian Tunnelling company. This party sustained casualties just as it was reaching its destination with its load. Throughout enfiladed the old German where the companies were with an H.V. gun and did some field gun sniping. He also shelled in the neighbourhood of Spoil Bank. Casualties 1 OR killed 3 wounded. [illegible] 2nd Lt Copied from 2nd Lt F Bourne	

A6945 Wt. W11422/M1160 350,000 12/16 D. D. & L. Forms/C./2118/14.

Instructions regarding War Diaries and Intelligence Summaries are contained in F. S. Regs., Part II, and the Staff Manual respectively. Title pages will be prepared in manuscript.

WAR DIARY
or
INTELLIGENCE SUMMARY.
(Erase heading not required.)

Army Form C. 2118.

Place	Date	Hour	Summary of Events and Information	Remarks and references to Appendices
Norfolk Road	27.6.17		During the morning orders were received to the effect that this Batt had to relieve the 10 R. W. Kent Regiment in the sector it has left on the 23rd. C coy took the left front line. D the right including the strong point. A coy took the new support line dug by them the night of the 22nd west in front of OPAL reserve on the right of the C.T. B coy was in in our old front line at the top of Estaminet lane. The whole of A, C and D coys garrisoned the line by night. At Dawn the garrison was reduced to 4 L.G. teams (5 men each) with 4 bombers attached to each team per coy. 1 Vickers gun in the strong point and one in the support line this gun was knocked out on the morning of the 29th. Added to this one L.G. (5 men) with 4 bombers from B coy behind A coy in the old support line. The whole garrison returning at night for work. The enemy shelled White Chateau wood and our lines at intervals during the day, after paying special attention to Spoil bank during the morning. The relief was duly carried out. Casualties 4 OR killed [illegible]	
Norfolk Rd	28.6.17		From 2.30 AM to 3.30 AM our Artillery heavily shelled OBLIQUE trench the enemy replied with a few Whizzbangs, which fell between our front and S line. Our S line and White CHATEAU wood was again intermittently shelled. A few bombs were thrown at our bombing post. Patrol report attached. Casualties 1 OR's killed.	2/LT. P.F. LARGE

A6945 Wt. W11422/M1160 350,000 12/16 D. D. & L. Forms/C./2118/14.

Army Form C. 2118.

Instructions regarding War Diaries and Intelligence Summaries are contained in F. S. Regs., Part II. and the Staff Manual respectively. Title Pages will be prepared in manuscript.

WAR DIARY
or
INTELLIGENCE SUMMARY
(Erase heading not required.)

Place	Date	Hour	Summary of Events and Information	Remarks and references to Appendices
Norfolk Road	29.6.17		Early in the morning the enemy shelled our old support line and the wood in rear. Later and in the afternoon our new support line. Early in the morning a few trench bombs were thrown at our strong point. At about 7 AM four enemy planes flew very low over our strong point. They were engaged by our M.G. Several pieces of an enemy plane fell from a great height about 200x in front of our line. The black cross being distinctly visible on some of the pieces. The weather continued wet rendering the ground very bad for movement and the trenches extremely muddy, except the new support line, the condition of which was far better than in the other trenches. ~~Patrol report attached~~. Casualties 4 OR killed 6 OR wounded NIL [illegible]	Appendix V Strength State attached
Norfolk Rd	30.6.17		At 2 AM our artillery which had been active at 11 PM 29th inst put a barrage on OBLIQUE trench and OPTIC support. Shortly before this some firing took place well to our left started by the enemy with a sharp barrage. Many and varied lights were sent up by him. During the morning there was slight intermittent shelling on both sides. Between 1 and 2 PM the enemy sent over a large number of whizzbangs slightly in front of and behind our front line. He also dropped two shells in our own trench near our S.P. The wood and our S line were shelled during the afternoon. The Battn was relieved on the night of 30.6.17 & 1.7.17 by the 23rd London Regt 47th Divn. Their officers had been taken round the line in the morning and guides were at OAK dump at 10 PM to conduct companies up the line. Heavy rain fell during the evening and a drizzle continued well into the night. This rendered the going in the dark very slow especially near the canal bank where several men had to be pulled out of the mud. Relief was completed early on the morning of the 1st 7th 17. Casualties 5 OR wounded NIL [illegible]	P.T.O.

G M McNicoll Major
Commdg. 20th Durham L.I.

Appendix I.

List of captured
Material &c. 7. 6. 1917.

Machine Guns & Telescopic sights complete	2
Search light complete	1
Rocket firer	1
Medium Trench Mortar	1
Compressed Air Helmet	1
Rifles & equipment.	Large quantity.

~~Search light~~

[signature] Lt
I.O.

7.6.17

Instructions regarding War Diaries and Intelligence Summaries are contained in F. S. Regs., Part II. and the Staff Manual respectively. Title pages will be prepared in manuscript.

123/41

Army Form C. 2118.

WAR DIARY
or
~~INTELLIGENCE SUMMARY.~~

(Erase heading not required.) 10th Durham Light Infantry

Vol 15

Place	Date	Hour	Summary of Events and Information	Remarks and references to Appendices
In the trenches MURRUMBIDGEE CAMP	1.7.17.		During the night of June 30th – July 1st the Battalion was relieved by the 23rd London Regt of the 47th Div. Relief was complete by 3am. The Battalion has been in the line since the 6th. Breakfasts were served on return to camp; the men afterward slept till 3pm when dinners were served prior to proceeding by march route to MONT DES CATS at 5.30pm. We arrived at our billets about 10.30pm. Only 5 men fell out on the march. Weather fine. Casualties nil. PHLox	
MONT DES CATS	2.7.17		The day was spent in reequipping & rest. Weather fine. PHLox. 2/LT. SMITH E and draft of 234 OR's reported	
— " —	3.7.17		Coys did 1 hours close order drill during the morning, after which platoon commanders reorganized their platoons. The Draft was distributed between Coys, nearly all of the men have served with the E.F before. Weather fine. PHLox	
— " —	4.7.17.		Classes of instruction in map reading, Lewis Gunnery, Musketry, & Drill were started for officers & N.C.O's. Remainder of the Battn were doing gas drill, rapid loading, Drill etc. Weather, fine. PHLox	
— " —	5.7.17.		Coys marched in turn to the baths some four miles off. Training was carried out as on the 4th. CAPT N.E. SIM left for 3 months course at ALDERSHOT. Weather fine. PHL	
— " —	6.7.17.		Coys were firing on the Range. Special attention was paid to Rapid fire. There were a good many enemy aircraft in vicinity of BAILLEUL to-day. Weather fine. Draft of 115 arrived from 2/7th D.L.I. PHLox Lt.	
— " —	7.7.17		During the night of 6th–7th enemy aircraft dropped bombs on BAILLEUL & HAZEBROUCKE. Coys carried out training under their own arrangements. PHLox Lt. Weather fine.	Strength State attached
— " —	8.7.17		Church parade was cancelled owing to rain. Sports in the afternoon. Weather dull. PHLox Lt.	
— " —	9.7.17.		Coys were at the baths & range, & trained till 12am. From 2.30–3.30 the Battn did ceremonial for the coming inspection by GENERAL LAWFORD. Weather fine. PHLox Lt.	

(A7092). Wt. W12839/M1293. 750,000. 1/17. D. D. & L., Ltd. Forms/C.2118/14.

Instructions regarding War Diaries and Intelligence Summaries are contained in F. S. Regs., Part II. and the Staff Manual respectively. Title pages will be prepared in manuscript.

WAR DIARY
~~or~~
~~INTELLIGENCE SUMMARY.~~
(Erase heading not required.) 10th Durham Light Infantry

Army Form C. 2118.

Place	Date	Hour	Summary of Events and Information	Remarks and references to Appendices
MONT DES CATS.	10.7.17.		The Bn. again practiced ceremonial. For the remainder of the day Coys trained in Musketry, drill, outposts etc. Weather fine. RHloa	
— " —	11.7.17.		At 9.am the Battn. were formed up in mass for inspection & presentation of medal ribbon by MAJ. Gen LAWFORD. The Bn. were practiced in Drill, Musketry, & extended order, after which the presentation took place. The Gen expressed his satisfaction at what he had seen, & urged the older soldiers in the Bn. to tell the new drafts what a great name the Bn. had made for itself. Sports were held in the afternoon. Weather fine. RHloa	List of Awards to this Battalion attached
— " —	12.7.17		Coy training in Musketry. Attack formations. Rifle grenade work etc. Weather fine. RHloa	
— " —	13.7.17		Battn. Drill was carried out at 8am, after which Coy training & the worst shots in the Bn. went to the Range for instruction. Weather fine. RHlowler	
— " —	14.7.17.		Same programme as on 13th. Weather fine. RHlowler	Strength State attached
— " —	15.7.17		The Brigadier inspected all Drafts men who have arrived since 7th June. Brigade Sports in the afternoon in which this Battn. was the most successful unit. Weather fine. RHloa	
— " —	16.7.17		The Battn. marched to ~~the~~ C. Corps parade ground ~~Area~~ & carried out a practice ~~attack~~. In forming up on tapes the 1st, 3rd & 5th waves were mixed in rafts ~~Although the going was bad~~ it proved an excellent lesson for the following day. Weather fine. RHloa. A most exciting Section Shooting Competition was held to-day & won by A Coy. RHloa	
— " —	17.7.17		A & D Coys practiced on the Range with falling iron plates & the "jumping Jimmy". B and C Coys carried out P.T, BT, & Musketry training. After this training the Bn. ~~again~~ practiced the attack on the 9th Corps Area. Weather fine. RHloa	
— " —	18.7.17		The whole Brigade did a practice attack to-day. Zero hour was at 6pm. The Brigadier expressed his satisfaction at the practice, though the Blue line in the shape of men with flags apparently lost their bearings. We returned to billets about 8.30pm owing to rain. Weather sultry. RHloa	
— " —	19.7.17		The Battn. paraded in turn for bath two miles off. Officers & N.C.O's proceeded to RENINGHELST in the evening to view a model of the ground over which the Battn. is to attack. Weather fine. RHloa The M.O arranged a stretcher bearing Competition which was a great success.	

(A7092). Wt. W12839/M1293. 750,000. 1/17. D. D. & L., Ltd. Forms/C.2118/14.

Army Form C. 2118.

Instructions regarding War Diaries and Intelligence Summaries are contained in F. S. Regs., Part II. and the Staff Manual respectively. Title pages will be prepared in manuscript.

WAR DIARY

~~or~~

~~INTELLIGENCE SUMMARY.~~

(Erase heading not required.)

20th Durham Light Infantry

Place	Date	Hour	Summary of Events and Information	Remarks and references to Appendices
MONT DES CATS	20.7.17		After Bath parade from 8am–9am, a gas demonstration was held for the men of the last two drafts. At 2pm the 123. Brigade were formed up in a hollow square for the presentation of medal ribbon to Col. WOOD MARTIN DSO who commands the 10 R.W. Kents in our Brigade. Gen. Lawford after the presentation, congratulated the Brigade on their steadiness on parade. A Pontoon Drill competition was held afterwards in which No 6 Pontoon were 3rd in the absence of its commander 2/Lt CARTWRIGHT. Weather fine. P.H.Lox. 2/Lt RUSSELL reported for duty & is posted to C. Coy.	
KENORA CAMP WESTOUTRE.	21.7.17.		The Bn moved to KENORA CAMP leaving MONT DES CATS at 10.10am, after 3 weeks rest: the feature of the training was the extraordinary keenness shown by the Bn in all the competitions which the Commanding Officer organized. The men were in billets by 2.15pm. Weather fine. P.H.Lox	Strength State attached
— " —	22.7.17.		The Bn were formed up for Church parade at 11am. In the evening each Coy practiced forming up on tapes. Weather fine. P.H.Lox.	
— " —	23.7.17		The Bn paraded in the evening for a practice in forming up on tapes. During the morning Coys held a kit inspection to see that they were perfectly ready to go into action. GENERAL GORDON & CAPTAIN PRAGNELL (Bde Major) were killed to-day near the bluff. Weather fine. P.H.Lox	
— " —	24.7.17		At 3.30pm the Bn moved to WOOD CAMP. A party of officers & selected men attended the funeral of the Brigadier & Brigade Major who were buried at RENINGHELST. Weather fine. P.H.Lox.	
WOOD CAMP to TRENCHES.	25.7.17		At 2 pm the Battalion left WOOD CAMP and marched to RIDGE WOOD where they bivouaced for tea. From thence they marched up into the line via SPOIL BANK & RAVINE WOOD. C Coy holding 3 advanced posts. D Coy in support in RAVINE in FUSILIER WOOD. B Coy close by the CATERPILLAR and A Coy in Reserve in RAVINE WOOD. Battalion HQ were in the CATERPILLAR. Casualties. Wounded O.R. 4 L.W. Shepherdson	
TRENCHES	26.7.17		Nothing unusual to report. Casualties Killed O.R. 2. Wounded O.R. 1 Missing O.R. 5	

(A7092). Wt. W12839/M1293. 750,080. 1/17. D. D. & L., Ltd. Forms/C.2118/14.

Army Form C. 2[illegible]

Instructions regarding War Diaries and Intelligence Summaries are contained in F. S. Regs., Part II. and the Staff Manual respectively. Title pages will be prepared in manuscript.

WAR DIARY
~~or~~
~~INTELLIGENCE SUMMARY.~~

(Erase heading not required.) 20th Durham Light Infantry

Place	Date	Hour	Summary of Events and Information	Remarks and references to Appendices
In the Trenches	July 27th		News being received that the attack which was expected for the 28th was indefinitely postponed, it was decided that Companies in turn should occupy the Strong Points to acquaint them with the Assembly Area for the assault. Accordingly on the evening of the 27th, A Coy took over from C, C Coy from D, D Coy from B and B Coy from A, the two front Coys being placed under the command of Capt Humphrey as O.C. Front Area, with his HQ in the RAVINE in FUSILIER WOOD. Later in the night, on information being received that the enemy was evacuating his front opposite 5th Army, B Coy also was placed under Capt. Humphrey, with 2 Vickers Guns and 2 Stokes Mortars to occupy the enemy lines opposite if necessary. Patrols however reported enemy opposite were not evacuating their lines. Casualties:- Killed O.R. 1. Missing O.R. 1. Wounded O.R. 12	
-do-	28th		Companies again moved round one place in the above order with the exception that A Coy owing to heavy shelling in FUSILIER WOOD, left only their Lewis Gunners there. The remainder of the Coy were withdrawn to CATERPILLAR AREA. Casualties:- 2/Lt C.R. Walker (attd R.E.s) Killed. 5 O.R. Killed 32 O.R. wounded (includes 8 gassed) 1 O.R. missing	Strength State attached SWS
-do-	29th		Companies again moved round one place. Lewis Gunners of Support Coy only remaining in the RAVINE in FUSILIER WOOD. It was decided, to enable tapes to be laid out quietly, that no more Company reliefs would take place. Capt Humphreys 2/Lt Shepherdson & 2/Lt Walton reconnoitred the Assembly Area in the afternoon, and the two former on the night 29/30th, laid out string to mark the position of the tapes and in so doing encountered an enemy patrol with whom they exchanged fire. Casualties. 42 O.R. wounded (includes 36 gassed) SWS	

(A7092). Wt. W12839/M1293. 750,000. 1/17. D. D. & L., Ltd. Forms/C.2118/14.

Instructions regarding War Diaries and Intelligence Summaries are contained in F. S. Regs., Part II. and the Staff Manual respectively. Title pages will be prepared in manuscript.

WAR DIARY

~~or~~

~~INTELLIGENCE SUMMARY.~~ 10th Durham Light Infantry

(*Erase heading not required.*)

Army Form C. 2

Place	Date	Hour	Summary of Events and Information	Remarks and references to Appendices
In the Trenches	30th July		As it appeared probable that the attack would take place next day, Capt Humphrey reported at Battn and 2/Lt Shepheardson that evening replaced the string with tape on the Assembly Area. Orders being received that Zero hour was 3.50 am on the 31st Coys moved up to the Assembly Area on the evening of the 30th, sustaining a certain number of casualties on the way from enemy barrage, which during the last few days had been very active across and in rear of FUSILIER WOOD. Casualties: Killed OR 1. Wounded OR 15 (includes 1 gassed)	
— do.	31st July		Before Zero the Battalion was formed up in 5 waves on a two Company front each on a two platoon front. Each Company had two platoons in its ~~[illegible]~~ leading wave and the third platoon as a Carrying & Mopping ~~[illegible]~~ platoon in its second wave. Battn formed the 5th wave. C Coy was on the left with A Coy behind them, and D Coy on the right with B Coy behind, the left flank of the left Company resting on the KLEIN - ZILLEBEKE ROAD, and the right flank of the right Coy in touch with the 10th Bn R W Kent Regt. The first ~~[illegible]~~ two waves were to assault the enemy front line, IMPERFECT TRENCH (RED LINE). The second were to mop it up and afterwards go forward to dig Strong Points. The R.E. were intended to consolidate this line but did not do so while the Battalion was there. The second wave supported by 3rd 4th & 5th waves were to assault and mop up the enemy second line. The 3rd & 4th waves were to pass through them and dig in a GREEN LINE under a protective barrage some 400 yards further on. The Red Line was to be the line of resistance, the Green Line sited for observation and the Blue Line to be the Support Line to it. The front line was successfully taken by assault in face of heavy shell fire and machine gun fire from concealed dugouts which the Artillery had not destroyed. The Battalion then advanced and dug in on the Blue Line and slightly in front of it, being able to get no further. Capt & Adjt Wagman	

(A7092). Wt. W12839/M1293- 75,0080. 1/17. D. D. & L., Ltd. Forms/C.2118/14.

Instructions regarding War Diaries and Intelligence Summaries are contained in F. S. Regs., Part II. and the Staff Manual respectively. Title pages will be prepared in manuscript.

Army Form C. 2118.

WAR DIARY
or
~~INTELLIGENCE~~ SUMMARY. 20th Durham Light Infantry.

(*Erase heading not required.*)

Place	Date	Hour	Summary of Events and Information	Remarks and references to Appendices
In the Trenches	31-7-17		was killed. 2/Lieut Fletcher O.C. D Coy, 2/Lt Clark, D Coy were wounded. 2/Lt Russell C Coy sprained his ankle while on the way to the Assembly Area and Capt Hand, O.C. C Coy pushed forward too far with some of his men and was not heard of again - Missing believed killed. Lieut Cox proceeding to take the place of Capt Wayman was wounded close to Bn H.Q. and 2/Lt Walton taking over Capt Wayman's place was killed shortly afterwards. Capt Fullgames O.C. B Coy was wounded near the Blue Line leaving 2/Lt Lacy in command. 2/Lt Britton O.C. A Coy was killed near the Blue Line leaving 2/Lt Smith in command. The Battalion was then disposed roughly on or about the Blue Line. A Coy on the left flank, B Coy on their right Details of C & D Coys on the right of B Coy ~~[illegible]~~ in touch with ~~[illegible]~~ the 10th Bn Kents, but not in touch with B Coy. Casualties by this time were very heavy owing to concealed nests of German Snipers, Machine Gunners & Bombers in concrete dugouts near the Blue Line. A & B Coys eventually cleared most of these at a heavy cost and Colonel North himself directing operations against other such positions was wounded. In the afternoon of the 31st the enemy counter attacked on the left of the line at the time Col. North was wounded and Capt Humphrey went up and took over command despatching 2/Lt Shepherdson to bring up 2 Coys of the 11th Bn K.R.R.C who were in support. These he placed in the gap between B Coy & the details of C & D Coys. The whole of the Assembly Area, No Man's Land and captured ground and FUSILIER WOOD was at this time under heavy and continuous barrages of Howitzer & Field Gun fire, while No Man's Land & the captured ground were enfiladed from right and left by machine gun fire. Capt Humphrey called on the Artillery for S.O.S. through the Visual Station of the R.W. Kents on the flank of the Assembly Area and the Artillery fire, together with rifle and Lewis Gun fire from the Blue Line and from a Vickers Gun which had succeeded in getting up to our left flank forward positions, smashed up the counter attack.	

(A7092). Wt. W12839/M1293. 750,000. 1/17. D. D. & L., Ltd. Forms/C.2118/14.

Army Form C. 2[illegible].

Instructions regarding War Diaries and Intelligence Summaries are contained in F. S. Regs., Part II. and the Staff Manual respectively. Title pages will be prepared in manuscript.

WAR DIARY
or
~~INTELLIGENCE~~ SUMMARY. 10th Durham Light Infantry
(Erase heading not required.)

Place	Date	Hour	Summary of Events and Information	Remarks and references to Appendices
In the Trenches	31-7-1917		The night was quiet, though small parties of the enemy were continually attempting to bomb our forward positions	
			Casualties. Officers - Killed 3, Wounded 5, Missing believed Killed 1.	
			O.R. - Killed 18, Wounded 153 (includes 9 gassed) Missing 73	
			2/Lieuts J Corbett & W Bannerman reported for duty from 3rd D.L.I.	
			S W Shepherdson	
			R C Smith Major	

(A7092). Wt. W12839/M1293. 750,000. 1/17. D. D. & L., Ltd. Forms/C.2118/14.

SECRET Appendix VI Copy No.

20th Durham Light Infantry Operation Order No 88
by Lt. Col. P. W. North

Ref. Maps Sheets 28 NW + 28 SW 1/10000

1 INTENTION The Battalion is to be ready to take part in the forthcoming operations at short notice after 31st May 1917. The 41st Divisional Frontage of attack will be from DIEPENDAAL BEEK to UPPER OOSTHOEK FM. The frontage allotted to 123rd Inf. Bde will be from SHELLEY FARM to O.3 d 45 90. This Battalion, less C Coy, will form the last waves (y + z) of the attack. C Coy will be distributed as moppers-up between the 3 assaulting Battalions.

2. DISPOSITION OF DIVISIONS

On the Right - 124th Inf Bde
" " Left - 123rd Inf Bde.
Divisional Reserve - 122nd Inf Bde R.E's, Pioneers.

3. DISPOSITION OF BRIGADE.

On the Right - 23rd Bn. Middlesex Regt
In centre - 10th R.W. Kent Regt
On the left - 11th Bn Queens
In Support - 20th Durham L. I.

4. DISPOSITION OF BATTALION Disposition of Coys two hours before Zero – Boundaries and objectives have already been issued accompanied by maps "A" & "B".

5. DAYS PREVIOUS TO ATTACK The attack will take place on Zero day after several days preliminary bombardment. Zero day will be referred to as "Z" day and the 5 preceding days as "Y" "X" "W" "V" "U". The days before "U" will be known as Z minus 6, Z minus 7 etc. Days after Z day as "A" "B" "C" days. After "C" day as Z plus 4, Z plus 5 etc.

6 PROCEEDING OF ATTACK. The Battalion will line out and be in position in its Assembly Area 2 hours before Zero.
The Battalion will be formed up thus – C Coy, less 4 Lewis Guns & Teams will be units to which it is attached, A, B & D Coys each in two waves forming the last waves (7 & 8) of the attack and in rear of the Right, Centre and Left Battalions respectively. Bn HQ together with 4 Lewis Guns of C Coy will follow 25 yds behind the 8th wave in rear of B Coy. The Machine Gun Coy detachment will have two Vickers Guns on the right & 2 on the left of Bn HQ. The Stokes Gun Detachment will

to be in the left of the 3 Vickers Guns on the left of Bn HQ.
The first waves will move up from their positions in the Assembly Area in sufficient time to get within 75 yds of the enemy parapet by Zero hour. This Battalion will move forward accordingly. At Zero plus 3 mins the artillery will lift off the enemy front line and at that moment the leading wave will attack followed by the whole Brigade. The first wave will halt in the enemy's Support Line with its section of moppers-up from C Coy, who will deal with the line quickly + thoroughly and immediately on entry.
The remainder of the Brigade will continue to move forward. When the 7th + 8th waves, composed of this Battalion reach the enemy support + front lines respectively, half of each wave will remain to mop them up and half will push forward at least 60 yds in advance of these lines where they will dig in as previously ordered. As soon as the 7th wave reaches the enemy's support line (the line close in front of EIKHOFF FARM and not the ruinous trench between that and the enemy's front line) the first wave will reform and follow the attack after handing the progress report of the "mopping" so that the mopping-up party in the 7th wave can have the line properly in hand.
The moppers up from C Coy accompanying the second wave will, after mopping-up the enemy front line, remain there in Battalion Reserve, the Officer in Charge of them reporting to the Adjutant

at Bn HQ as soon as the mopping up is complete. The moppers up accompanying the 1st wave, will as soon as the mopping up is complete, report to the nearest O/c Coy. As soon as possible after dark these men will be collected and sent to rejoin their Coy as Batn Reserve in the Front Line, the Senior Officer in the Coy reorganising it.

Bombs and other material, of which further particulars will be issued later, will be left by the 5th wave in the enemy support line as it passes through. This material will be collected and stored into dumps by A, B + D Coys. at the earliest possible moment, each Coy making two dumps in its sector on the parapet of the trench.

At Zero plus 35 mins the barrage will move forward from in front of the Red Line and waves 2, 3 4, 5 + 6 will follow it and proceed straight to the final objective of this attack, the DAMMSTASSE.

Bn HQ will in all probability be near RUINED FARM.

All ranks in the Batn. are to know that the first duty of this Bn. after Zero plus 3 mins is to go straight forward, carrying with them the troops in front of them until they reach the enemy front + support lines. This is to be done without a stop and on arrival there the trenches will be mopped and a new trench dug in front of each. After reaching that objective the Bn may be used to take the DAMMSTRASSE if other units are held up, or later on may be used to help the Bde on our right. But from Zero plus 3 mins till we get in the enemy front & support lines their sole duty is to push on without stopping whether the people in front stop or not.

STRONG POINTS A Coy will establish 2 Strong Points at O.3.c 4.0 & O.3.c 8.3 and D Coy will establish 2 at O 3 d. 3.5 & O 3. d. 65.40. In each of these Strong Points will go the Vickers Gun previously detailed and a garrison consisting of one section from A & D Coys. B Coy will detail a party to dig a STRONG Point at EIKHOF FARM.

8. ARTILLERY TIME TABLE

Zero plus 3 mins	–	Front Line
" " 20 "	–	Support Line
" " 45 "	–	DAMMSTRASSE

9. MACHINE GUNS 4 Machine Guns from the 123rd M G Coy will move with the last wave of this Battalion and will proceed to the STRONG Points and dig them. Other Vickers Guns will be employed on the Bde front for barrage fire

10. STOKES GUNS The 123rd L T M B is bombarding the enemy front line trenches

on the Bde. Front from Zero to Zero plus one minute and the enemy support line from Zero plus one to Zero plus 3 minutes. After this one gun and team will come under the command of the Commanding Officer and will advance with H.Q. moving on left of the Vickers Guns on the left of Bn H.Q.

11. R.E. attached to BRIGADE One section of the 233rd Field Coy R.E. with the Pioneer Platoon from each Battalion is being sent up in organised parties to assist in the construction of Strong Points mentioned in Para 7. Should any arrive and not know where to go they are to be directed to the Strong Points.

12. Smoke & Gas There will be smoke & Gas barrages if the wind is favourable

13. ACTION ON EITHER FLANK The 124th Bde will attack on our right and the 140th Bde on our left. If either of these is held up O.s/c A & D Coys are to protect their respective outer flanks.

14. 122nd Bde ATTACK This Bde is taking the Black Line and is forming up in rear of DAMMSTRASSE by Zero plus 3 hours,

7

The attack commencing at Zero plus 3 hours 40 mins

15. ATTACK BY RESERVE DIVISION The Reserve Division 24th Division will continue the attack at Zero plus 10 hrs their objective being the Green Line running from O.10 b 7.7. to O.16. c 5.1.

16. TANKS 2 Sections of Tanks will accompany the advance.

17. MINES A mine will be exploded at Zero hour under Nos 2 & 3 CRATERS. Danger radius 200 yds. All Tunnelled dug outs will be evacuated until the explosion has occurred.

18. DRESS. Fighting ~~Order~~ Kit as previously ordered. Bomb buckets will be issued to Coys shortly.

19. Rations & DRESS Rations for Z & A days and water for 'X' & 'Y' days are on the Battalion Dump at H.29 d. 90 35. The following are water supplies which may be drawn on if necessary.
I 31 d.2 5   I 31 d 5 9.

20. AMMUNITION. There will be 3 reserve Ammunition Dumps in our present front line, positions of [illegible]

which will be issued as soon as known.

21. SYNCHRONIZATION OF WATCHES The Sig. Officer will arrange to have all watches Synchronised daily after 'X' day.

22. DISPOSITION REPORTS DISPOSITION REPORTS will all be rendered whenever possible on Sketch maps as previously Ordered. A fresh report to be rendered frequently and always when the enemy position changes.

23. MEDICAL The M.O will establish a Regimental aid Post at I 32. c. 5. 0½. As soon as the situation permits, the R.A.P. will be pushed forward to a point which will be notified later.

24 ~~31-5-17~~ Acknowledge

31-5-17 Issued by Runner at

Copies to:

No 1 C.O
2 O/c A Coy
3 O/c B Coy
4 O/c C Coy
5 O/c D Coy
6 Sig Officer
7 I.O
8 Q.M
9 M.O
10 11 Bn Queens
11 10 Bn R.W. Kents
12 23rd Middlesex

[signature] Lt
Adjutant
20th Durham L.I.

Appendix III

20th Durham L.I.
Daily State

	Off's	O.R's	Tot
Present in Trenches with Coys	17	508	525
do H.Q.	6	55	61
Transport Section	1	50	51
Q.M. Est.	1	16	17
Second Army	—	7	7
X Corps H.Q.	—	1	1
Div Employ	2	9	11
Bde do	1	19	20
Att'd to A.S.C.	—	1[illegible]	1[illegible]
do T.M.B.	—	14	14
do M.G.C.	—	1	1
Divl Sig Coy	—	23	23
Bde Rein Camp	—	1	1
Details left with Transport	2	12	14
Courses of Instr.	2	6	8
F.A. & D.R.S.	2	20	22
Traffic Control	—	4	4
Pigeon Personnel	—	3	3
On Leave	1	7	8
233 Field Coy R.E.	1	26	27
Rest Camp	1	13	14
Trade Test	—	2	2
Hutting Work	—	7	7
D.A.D.O.S.	—	1	1
Water Pt.	—	2	2
Absentee	—	1	1
16.5.17	37	811	848

Appendix IV

20th Durham L I
Daily State

	Offs	ORs	Tot
Present with Coys in Trenches	15	459	474
do HQ do	5	41	46
Transport Section	1	50	57
Details left behind	1	57	58
At Transport Lines	2	21	23
2nd Army	–	7	7
Xth Corps	–	1	1
Divl Employ	2	9	11
Bde do	1	20	21
Attd to A S C	–	1	1
do T M B	–	17	17
Divl Hq Coy	–	23	23
233rd Field Coy	1	26	27
Courses of Instn.	2	3	5
FA & D R S	2	33	35
On Leave	2	9	11
Rest Camp	–	7	7
Pigeon Personnel	–	3	3
Traffic Control	–	4	4
Hutting Work	–	7	7
D. A. D. O. S	–	1	1
Trades Test	–	2	2
Absentees	–	1	1
TOTAL	34	783	817

23-6-17

Appx 5. 20 Durham L.I.

Daily State.

	Offs.	ORS	TOT.
Present in Trenches with Coys	11	361	372
do H.Q.	5	44	49
At Transport Lines (Sick)	2	24	26
Transport Section	1	47	48
Q. Masters Est.	1	17	18
Second Army	–	7	7
Xth Corps Employ	–	1	1
Divl Employ	2	8	10
Bde Employ	1	23	24
Attd to A.S.C.	–	1	1
do T.M.B	–	17	17
do Divl Sig. Coy.	–	–	–
Courses of Instruction	2	12	14
F.A & D.R.S.	3	27	30
Traffic Control	–	4	4
Pigeon Personnel	–	3	3
On Leave	3	8	11
233rd Field Coy RE	1	26	27
Rest Camp	–	4	4
Trade Test	–	2	2
Hutting Work	–	6	6
D.A.D.O.S.	–	1	1
Water Pt	–	4	4
Billeting Party	2	6	8
Hospital with Officer	–	1	1
Details left behind	1	83	84
TOTAL.	35	837	872

30.6.17

LIST OF AWARDS.

MILITARY CROSS.

CAPTAIN. W. C. BROWN.
2/Lieut. W.R. Brook.
2/ Lieut. B. WILKINSON.

MILITARY MEDAL.

No. I6/25903 Sgt. W.McPHERSON.
No. I5586 Cpl W.H. HARE.
No. 20/62 Pte. T.H.S. MATHIESON.
No. 20/249 Pte. J. PARKIN.
No. 28420. Pte. E. BEST.
No. 2/634 Pte. J.J. BETTERIDGE.
No. 20/76 Pte. B. FENWICK.
No. 20/634 Pte. M. QUINN.
No. I053. Pte. J. HARRIS.
No.. I9I88. Pte. L. KINSTON.

JUNE 7th I9I7.
MESSINES.

I3I

20th (S) Bn Durham L. Inf.

Daily State

	Offs	O Ranks	Total
Present in Billets with Unit	17	753	770
— do — H.Qrs	4	59	63
Masterbrasters Establishment	1	16	17
2nd Army		7	7
10th Corps H.Qrs		1	1
Divl Employ	2	5	7
Bde do	2	17	19
Att A.S.C.		1	1
L.T.M. Battery		17	17
Courses of Instruction	2	18	20
In F.A + D.R.S.	2	24	26
Traffic Control		3	3
Pigeon Personnel		3	3
2nd Army Rest Camp		8	8
On Leave	2	12	14
Att to 233rd R.E.s	1	24	25
Trade Test		2	2
DADOS		1	1
Amm Dump Reninghelst	1	46	47
Divl Guard		8	8
Transport Section	1	45	46
	35	1070	1105

7/7/17

20th (S) Bn. Durham L. Infantry
Daily State

	Offs	ORs	Total
Present with Coys in Billets	17	792	809
do Hqrs do	6	65	71
Quarter Masters Estab.	1	15	16
Transport Section	1	45	46
2nd Army Hqrs		7	7
10th Corps. do		1	1
Divl Employ	2	4	6
Bde do		11	11
Att to A.S.C.		1	1
.. Tn Battery		17	17
Courses of Instruction	1	14	15
F.A. HRS.	1	12	13
Traffic Control		2	2
Pigeon Personnel		3	3
Rest Camp		11	11
Leave	4	18	22
Att to 233rd Field Coy R.E.s	1	24	25
Trade Test		1	1
D.A.D.O.S.		1	1
Divl Guard		8	8
	34	1052	1086

Aug 14/1917

20th (S) Bn Durham L. Infantry

Daily State

	Officers	O Ranks	Total
Present in Billets with Unit	15	725	740
do Hqrs	6	68	74
Transport Section	1	47	48
Quartermasters Establishment	1	15	16
Second Army		7	7
Xth Corps Hqrs		1	1
Divl Employ	2	4	6
Bde do		11	11
Att to A.S.C.		1	1
L. T.M. Battery		25	25
Machine Gun Co.		18	18
Courses of Instruction	1	14	15
G.A.A. D.R.S.	4	24	28
Traffic Control		–	–
Pigeon Personnel		3	3
On Leave	4	19	23
Attd to R.E's 233rd Field Coy	1	67	68
D.A.D.O.S.		1	1
Rest Camp		8	8
Trade Test		1	1
Hospital with Officer		1	1
	35	1060	1095

August 21st/1917

20th Bn Durham L.I.

Daily State

	Off	O.R.	Total
Present in Trenches with Unit	11	453	464
HQ	6	47	53
At Transport Lines Sick	-	2	2
Transport Section	1	47	48
Quartermasters Establishment	1	16	17
Second Army		7	7
X Corps Headquarters		1	1
Divisional Employ	2	4	6
Brigade Employ		11	11
Bde Salvage Officer	1	–	1
Attached to A.S.C		1	1
Attached to L.T.M. Battery		24	24
Attached to Machine Gun Coy.		17	17
Attached 26th Royal Fusiliers	1	1	2
Details left with Transport	4	203	207
Courses of Instruction	1	11	12
In Field Ambulance & D.R.S.	5	48	53
Traffic Control		1	1
Corps Lewis Gun Camp		3	3
Pigeon Personnel		3	3
On Leave	1	18	19
Attached to R.E.	1	32	33
Rest Camp		8	8
Trade Test		1	1
D.A.D.O.S.		1	1
Hospital with Officers		2	2
Absentees		2	2
568th Divnl R.E.		1	1
Brigade Runners		26	26
Total.	35	991	1026

28th July 1917

Instructions regarding War Diaries and Intelligence Summaries are contained in F. S. Regs., Part II. and the Staff Manual respectively. Title pages will be prepared in manuscript.

Army Form C. 2118.

Vol 16

WAR DIARY
or
~~INTELLIGENCE SUMMARY.~~
(Erase heading not required.)

20th Durham Light Infantry

Place	Date	Hour	Summary of Events and Information	Remarks and references to Appendices
In the Trenches	1-8-17		Towards dusk the enemy again formed up for counter attack but was dispersed by Artillery and rifle fire. On the night of 1/2nd the Battalion was relieved by 21st Bn K.R.R.C and marched back to BLUFF TUNNELS. Casualties: Officers missing 1 (2/Lt [illegible] Ballantyne) O.R. Killed 1. Wounded 34	
-do-	2-8-17		Day spent by men resting in BLUFF TUNNELS. Casualties — Killed O.R. 3 Wounded O.R. 22	
-do-	3-8-17		The Battalion marched from BLUFF TUNNELS to bivouac near ELZENWALLE CHATEAU at 4.30 am. The preceding 72 hours however had been heavy and continuous rain making movement very difficult. All ranks during the whole of this time had been soaked to the skin. Casualties Killed O.R. 1 Wounded O.R. 4 2/Lieut A.G. Dawson reported for Duty.	
-do-	4-8-17		Major R.C. Smith reported and took over Command of the Battalion. More Bivouacs were obtained and 2 Coys moved just S. of ELZENWALLE CHATEAU. Weather. Changeable. Much rain. Casualties Killed O.R. 1. Wounded O.R. 3	
-do-	5-8-17		The remaining 2 Coys had also moved to just S of ELZENWALLE CHATEAU and bivouaced. The men received dry underclothing and dried their service dress in the sun, the weather having changed. The Re-inforcements from the Re-inforcement Camp also joined the Battalion and were posted to Coys. The Battalion was re-organised on a two Company basis, 3 Platoons per Coy, A&C Coy being together + B&D Coys together	
-do-	6-8-17		The Battn relieved 26th Bn R.F in IMPERIAL SWITCH (support line.) Enemy Artillery very active, but relief successfully carried out. At 11.15 p.m. enemy shelled Battn Area very heavily using many gas shells. Weather changeable (wet) Casualties 1 O.R wounded.	

(A7092). Wt. W12839/M1293. 750,000. 1/17. D. D. & L., Ltd. Forms/C.2118/14.

Army Form C. 2118.

Instructions regarding War Diaries and Intelligence Summaries are contained in F. S. Regs., Part II. and the Staff Manual respectively. Title pages will be prepared in manuscript.

WAR DIARY
or
~~INTELLIGENCE SUMMARY.~~
(Erase heading not required.)

20th Durham Light Infantry

Place	Date	Hour	Summary of Events and Information	Remarks and references to Appendices
In the Trenches	7.8.17		Intermittent bombardment throughout the day, many gas shells sent over. RAVINE WOOD was shelled with 5.9 HOWITZERS. The weather, until the evening was very misty. Later on the mist cleared, and the 'planes of both sides became very active. Casualties 1 O.R. wounded [illegible] 68 O.R. Reinforcements arrived	
Do	8.8.17		At 3 a.m the enemy put up a heavy barrage, apparently expecting an attack at that hour. Throughout the day heavy counter battery work was carried out on both sides and Hostile Aircraft was very active. Casualties - wounded ORs 3. [illegible] 71 O.R. Reinforcements arrived	
Do	9.8.17		Batt: area shelled throughout the day with "whizz-bangs" and 4.2 How: but only one direct hit on our trenches. Great aerial activity throughout the day, at one time seven hostile machines flew over our lines very low, and remained in the vicinity for 15 minutes. Between 3 p.m and 4 p.m. an enemy balloon was brought down in flames, whilst another broke loose. A British balloon was also brought down in flames. Weather fine. Casualties killed 1 O.R. Wounded 1 O.R. [illegible] [illegible] T.E. [illegible] reported for duty	
Do	10.8.17		At 3.25 am a successfull attack was made by the Corps on the left of our Division. All objectives being gained. Our artillery very active throughout the day. Enemy Artillery exceptionally quiet. Great aerial activity on both sides. At 6 p.m the Batt: was relieved by the 32nd Batt R.F. and moved back to the RIDGEWOOD AREA. Weather fine. Casualties NIL. [illegible]	

(A7092). Wt. W12839/M1293. 750,000. 1/17. D. D. & L., Ltd. Forms/C.2118/14.

Instructions regarding War Diaries and Intelligence Summaries are contained in F. S. Regs., Part II. and the Staff Manual respectively. Title pages will be prepared in manuscript.

WAR DIARY
or
INTELLIGENCE SUMMARY.

(*Erase heading not required.*) 20th Battn Durham Light Infantry

Army Form C. 2118.

Place	Date	Hour	Summary of Events and Information	Remarks and references to Appendices
Ridge Wood	11·8·17		The day was spent in rest, and cleaning of equipment. A Brigade Silence was observed from 1·30 pm to 3·30 p.m. Capt G. D. Henderson 11th Batt R. W. Kent Regt attached temporarily to this Batt took over the duties of Acting Adjt from 2nd Lieut Shepherdson. A few shells dropped in the vicinity of the camp at night, but no casualties occurred. Weather wet. S	
Do	12·8·17		The Batt was conveyed by Motor Lorries to the METEREN AREA and encamped under canvass near FONTAINHOUCKE. Weather very hot. S	
FONTAINHOUCKE	13·8·17		The day was spent in re-organising the Batt on the 4 Coy. basis, and in general cleaning up. Weather wet. 68 OR Reinforcements arrived.	
"	14·8·17		The Batt paraded for close order drill, musketry, saluting drill etc in the morning. The afternoon being devoted to recreation, including a football match. S	
"	15·8·17		Parades exactly the same as the day before. In the afternoon 200 men proceeded to the Baths. Weather fine. Later in the Afternoon a draft of 52 men arrived S	
"	16·8·17		The Brigade was inspected by the Corps Commander, who expressed his thanks for the good work done by the 123rd Inf Bde during recent operations. Afterwards the remainder of the Batt went to the Baths and in the evening the first match of an inter-platoon football competition was played. S 155 OR Reinforcements arrived.	

(A7092). Wt. W12839/M1293- 750,080. 1/17. D. D. & L., Ltd. Forms/C.2118/14.

Army Form C. 2118.

WAR DIARY
or
~~INTELLIGENCE SUMMARY.~~
(Erase heading not required.) 20th Durham Light Infantry

Instructions regarding War Diaries and Intelligence Summaries are contained in F. S. Regs., Part II. and the Staff Manual respectively. Title pages will be prepared in manuscript.

Place	Date	Hour	Summary of Events and Information	Remarks and references to Appendices
FONTAIN HOUCKE	17.8.17		Coys at the disposal of Coy Commanders for the training of sections in the use of their respective weapons. Afternoon devoted to recreation. S	
"	18.8.17		Capt Crawford + 2/Lt [illegible] reported for duty. 84 OR reinforcements arrived. The Brigade was inspected by the Army Commander - Gen: Sir Herbert Plumer who complimented the men on the work done by them during recent operations. The rest of the day being a general holiday. S	
"	19.8.17		The Battalion paraded for Divine Service at 9.30 a.m. In the afternoon several matches of the inter-platoon football competition were played off. During the evening the Brigade band was in attendance, and the Battalion provided an enjoyable boxing contest. S	
"	20.8.17		The Battalion marched to STAPLES, a distance of 9 miles, on its way to the SOUTH TILQUES training area. S	
STAPLES	21.8.17		The march was completed to the final Billeting area. The area allotted to this Battalion being ESQUERDES. Today march was a distance of 17 miles, consequently the men were rather tired on arrival. S	
ESQUERDES	22.8.17		The day was devoted to rest and general cleaning up. Eight new officers reported for duty viz:- 2nd Lieuts Callow E.H., Pinkoe W.S., Oliver E.R., Cunningham C.S., Turnbull R.W., Smith R.P. Charlton R.J. and Whitfield H. S	

(A7092). Wt. W12839/M1293. 750,000. 1/17. D. D. & L., Ltd. Forms/C.2118/14.

Army Form C. 2[illegible].

Instructions regarding War Diaries and Intelligence Summaries are contained in F. S. Regs., Part II. and the Staff Manual respectively. Title pages will be prepared in manuscript.

WAR DIARY
or
~~INTELLIGENCE SUMMARY~~.
(Erase heading not required.) 20th Batt Durham L. I

Place	Date	Hour	Summary of Events and Information	Remarks and references to Appendices
Esquerdes	23.8.17		Battalion training carried out, Companies at the disposal of their Coy Commanders for the training of sections in the use of their respective weapons. S	
"	24.8.17		The division was inspected by the Field Marshall Commanding in Chief who complimented the troops on their smart appearance and handling of arms and also on the work done by them in the operations of the 31st July. After the inspection, the remainder of the day was observed as a general holiday. S	
"	25.8.17		Battalion drill under the Commanding Officer from 9 to 10 am. 10 am to 12.30 p m Company training. During the afternoon further matches of the inter-platoon football competition were played off. Under authority granted by H.M. the King, the Field Marshall Commanding in Chief, awarded the D.S.O to Lieut-Col P.W. North and the Military Cross to 2nd Lt J. M. Fletcher. S	
"	26.8.17		The Batt paraded for Divine Service at 10 a.m. The afternoon being devoted to football. S	
"	27.8.17		A + B Coys proceeded to the Training Area, C + D Coys trained on their Coy Ground, and went to the Baths in the afternoon. S	

(A7092). Wt. W12839/M1293. 750,000. 1/17. D. D. & L., Ltd. Forms/C.2118/14.

Army Form C. 2118.

Instructions regarding War Diaries and Intelligence Summaries are contained in F. S. Regs., Part II. and the Staff Manual respectively. Title pages will be prepared in manuscript.

WAR DIARY
or
~~INTELLIGENCE SUMMARY.~~

(Erase heading not required.) 20th Durham Light Infantry

Place	Date	Hour	Summary of Events and Information	Remarks and references to Appendices
ESQUERDES	28.8.17		A + B Coys proceeded to the range but had to return owing to the heavy rain. Training was carried on in Coy billets. Baths were allotted to A + B Coys from 2 to 4.30 p.m. SS	
"	29.8.17		Owing to the weather still remaining very wet, Coys were confined to billets for training. SS	
"	30.8.17		C + D Coys proceeded to the training area to carry out, Extended Order Drill Artillery formation etc. A B Coys, trained on their own parade grounds. Under Authority granted by H.M. the King, the Field Marshall Commanding in Chief awarded the Military Cross to the following officers: – Capt H F Wilson RAMC att. 20th DLI, a/Capt E Smith, 2/Lt J G R Bailey, and 2nd Lt L. W. Stephenson SS	
"	31.8.17		A + B Coys training on the training Area, C + D Coys training on their Coy parade grounds. Capt W C Brown MC took over the duties of Adjt from Capt G D Henderson MC R W Kent Regt. ~~who departed to Div HQrs for a Staff Course~~. L Stephenson	Course postponed R.C.

R C Smith Lt Col
Cmdg 20th D.L.I.

(A7092). Wt. W12839/M1293. 750,000. 1/17. D. D. & L., Ltd. Forms/C.2118/14.

20TH. BN. DURHAM LIGHT INFANTRY.

List of AWARDS for the month of AUGUST 1917.

Lieut.Col.P.W.North----The Distinguished Service Order.
Capt.H.F.Wilson.--------The Military Cross.
Capt.E.Smith. ---------- - do -
Lieut.T.M.Fletcher. --- - do -
2/Lieut.J.C.R.Pacy. ---- - do -
2/Lieut.L.W.Shepherdson. - do -
20/41 Sergt. A.Houston. The Distinguished Conduct Medal.
19/866. Sergt. D.Scott. The Military Medal.

20/485.L/C J Hannah. - do -
18189 L/C J Ramsden. - do -
42575 Pte.T.Yeomans. - do -
20/929 Pte. R.Dixon. - do -
20/681 Pte. E.Howard. - do -
22133 Pte. J.E.Thompson. - do -
20/558 Pte.E.Bell. - do -
204951 Pte.W.Mears. - do -
9081 Pte.J.H.Darrell. - do -
20/331 Pte.R.Mordey. - do -
32763 Pte.R.Ellison. - do -
12616 Pte.W.Burke. - do -
20/44 Pte.J.Kirkup. - do -

20th Bn. DURHAM L. I.

DAILY STATE

	OFF's	O.R's	TOTAL
Present in Billets with Coys.	22	746	768
do HQ.	5	74	79
Transport Section	1	47	48
Q.M. Establishment	1	18	19
2nd Army	–	1	1
Xth Corps Employ.	–	–	–
Divl Employ.	2	4	6
Bde do.	–	12	12
Attd to A.S.C.	–	1	1
do T.M.B.	–	16	16
Courses of Instruction	1	24	25
In FA & DRS.	4	26	30
On Leave	1	4	5
Pigeon Personnel.	–	3	3
Attd 233rd Field Coy RE.	–	23	23
Rest Camp.	1	5	6
Attd 26 Bn R F's.	1	1	2
D.A.D.O.S.	–	1	1
Attd 228th Field Coy R.E.	–	1	1
Trade Test.	–	1	1
Absentees.	–	2	2
TOTAL	39	1010	1049

26-8-17.

20th Bn. Durham L. I

Daily State

	Off	O.R's	Total
Present in Billets with Coys.	15	757	772
do H.Qrs	5	68	73
Transport Section	1	47	48
Q.M. Estab.	1	18	19
Second Army	–	1	1
X Corps Employ	–	1	1
Divisional do	2	4	6
Brigade do	–	13	13
Attd to A.S.C	–	1	1
do T.M.B.	–	15	15
Courses of Instruction	1	17	18
In F.A. & D.R.S.	3	25	28
Pigeon Personnel	–	3	3
On Leave	1	6	7
Attd to 233rd Field Coy R.E.	–	23	23
" 567 Devon R.E.	–	1	1
Rest Camp	1	5	6
Attd 26 Bn. R.F's	1	1	2
Dados	–	1	1
Absentees	–	2	2
Total	31	1009	1040

19-8-17

20th Bn Durham L I
DAILY STATE

	OFF	OR	TOTAL
Present in Trenches with Coys	9	263	272
do HQ.	4	40	44
Transport Section	1	48	49
Q.M. Estab	1	17	18
Second Army	–	3	3
X Corps. Employ	–	1	1
Divisional do	2	5	7
Brigade do	–	14	14
Attd to A.S.C	–	1	1
do T.M.B.	–	23	23
Course of Instruction	–	9	9
In FA & DRS.	3	81	83
Pigeon Personnel	–	3	3
On Leave	–	10	10
Attd 233 Field Coy. RE	–	24	24
Rest Camp	–	8	8
DADOS.	–	1	1
Trade Test	–	1	1
26th Bn. R F's.	1	1	2
Absentees		3	3
Attd M. G. Coy TOTAL	–	6	6
Details left behind	8	168	176
TOTAL STRENGTH	29	730	759

12-8-17

20th Bn. Durham L I

DAILY STATE

	OFF	OR	TOTAL
Present in Trenches with Coys	15	330	345
do HQrs.	3	27	30
Q. M Estab	1	16	17
Transport Section.	1	47	48
Second Army	–	3	3
X" Corps Employ	–	1	1
Divl Employ	2	4	6
Brigade "	–	11	11
Attd to A. S. C	–	1	1
T. M B	–	24	24
" M G C	–	17	17
Courses of Instruction	–	11	11
In FA & D R S	3	40	43
Traffic Control	–	1	1
Pigeon Personnel	–	3	3
On Leave	–	17	17
Attd 233 Field Coy RE	–	32	32
5th Devon Rt.	–	1	1
Rest Camp	–	8	8
Trade Test.	–	1	1
D. A D. O. S	–	1	1
Absentee	–	1	1
24th Bn. R F's.	1	1	2
Cord Lane Dump.	–	1	1
	26	599	625

5-8-17.

14

Instructions regarding War Diaries and Intelligence Summaries are contained in F. S. Regs., Part II. and the Staff Manual respectively. Title pages will be prepared in manuscript.

WAR DIARY or INTELLIGENCE SUMMARY.

(Erase heading not required.)

Army Form C. 2118.

20th Durham Light Infantry
for September 1917

123/41

Vol 17

Place	Date 1917	Hour	Summary of Events and Information	Remarks and references to Appendices
ESQUERDES (Pas-de-Calais)	Sept 1st		"A" & "B" Coys fired on "C" Range near CORMETTE after billetting there for the night 31st Aug/1st Sept. "C" & "D" Coys on small range at ESQUERDES and trained on Bn Ground. Lt (A/Capt.) W.C. BROWN promoted Captain from 2.3.1917. G.A.S. Lt.	
-do-	- 2nd		Church parade 11 am. Heats for Bn Sports took place in morning. Divisional Cross Country Run took place in afternoon won by 20th Durh L.I., 2nd 18th K.R.R. G.A.S. Lt.	
-do-	- 3rd		"C" & "D" Coys fired on "C" Range 10am – 1 pm. "A" & "B" Coys training on Bn Ground. The Bn Sports were held in the afternoon. *2nd Lt. W. HEBRON reported for duty. G.A.S. Lt.	
-do-	- 4th		Battalion in attack practised on training area near LEULINGHAM. Operation Order No. 1 and map attached as appendix I. G.A.S. Lt.	appendix I
-do-	- 5th		Battalion fired on new range near LUMBRES during whole day. A Liason practice was held with the R.F.C. near QUELMES. 2nd Lt. W.D. CLARK rejoined Bn from hospital today. G.A.S. Lt.	
-do-	- 6th		The Day, after 10 am, observed as a holiday owing to the Brigade Sports which were held near SETQUES. Brigade Championship won by 20th Durh L.I. 11th Queens second. G.A.S. Lt.	
-do-	- 7th		Brigade in attack practised on training area near ETREHEM in front of Army & Divl Commanders. Lecture on "Intelligence" at Divn HQ in afternoon. G.A.S. Lt.	
-do-	- 8th		Battalion trained by Coys in morning on training area. The Baths at SETQUES were allotted to half the Bn in the afternoon. The Divn Horse Show was held in the afternoon. The first party of 5 Officers went to reconnoitre the piece of line over which the Divn is to attack. G.A.S. Lt.	
-do-	- 9th		Church parade 9.45 am. The Baths at SETQUES were allotted to half the Bn in the afternoon. The second party of Officers reconnoitred the line near YPRES. G.A.S. Lt.	

(A7092). Wt. W12839/M1293. 750,000. 1/17. D. D. & L., Ltd. Forms/C.2118/14.

20th DLI
for September 1917.

Army Form C. 2118.

Instructions regarding War Diaries and Intelligence Summaries are contained in F. S. Regs., Part II. and the Staff Manual respectively. Title pages will be prepared in manuscript.

WAR DIARY
or
INTELLIGENCE SUMMARY.
(Erase heading not required.)

Place	Date 1917	Hour	Summary of Events and Information	Remarks and references to Appendices
ESQUERDES (Pas de Calais)	Sept. 10th		The Brigade practised an attack over a piece of ground similar to that over which the attack will be made in the line. GAB Lt.	
-do-	- 11th		The Battalion trained by Coys. on the training area. Live grenades were fired. GAB Lt.	
-do-	- 12th		The Battalion trained by Coys on the training area where live grenades were fired. A gas demonstration was given on the ground which the Bn attended. 2nd Lts. E. RUSSELL & R. H. ROBINSON joined the Bn for duty. GAB Lt.	
-do-	- 13th		The Battalion took part in a Brigade Practice attack over the same ground as on the 10th. Lieut. G. A. BAMLET took over the duties of Acting Adjutant from Captain W. C. BROWN who proceeded to hospital sick. GAB Lt.	
-do-	- 14th		The Battalion took part in a Brigade March to STAPLES. Route via WIZERNES - BLENDIQUES - WARDREQUES - EBBLINGHAM. Operation Order No 22 attached as Appendix II. GAB Lt.	Appendix II.
STAPLES.	- 15th		The Battalion continued in the Brigade March to PHINCBOOM. Route via CAISTRE - FLÊTRE. Operation Order No 23 attached as appendix III. GAB Lt.	Appendix III
PHINCBOOM	- 16th		The Battalion continued in the Brigade March to WESTOUTRE No 6 area and were accomodated in ALBERTA CAMP RENINGHELST. Route via LES 4 FILS AYMON - BERTHEN - MT. KOKEREELE - WESTOUTRE - RENINGHELST. Operation Order No 24 attached as appendix IV. Extracts from "Appointments, Commissions &c." Durham L.I. 2/Lt. B. WILKINSON to be Actg. Capt. whilst Commdg. a Company. 15th August 1917. The undermentioned to be Actg. Capts. (Additional) dated 15th August 1917. 2/Lt. E. SMITH 2/Lt. H. SOUTHWELL. GAB Lt.	Appendix IV

(A7092). Wt. W12839/M1293. 750,000. 1/17. D. D. & L., Ltd. Forms/C.2118/14.

20th Durham Light Infantry
for September 1917

Army Form C. 2118.

Instructions regarding War Diaries and Intelligence Summaries are contained in F. S. Regs., Part II. and the Staff Manual respectively. Title pages will be prepared in manuscript.

WAR DIARY
or
INTELLIGENCE SUMMARY.
(Erase heading not required.)

Place	Date 1917	Hour	Summary of Events and Information	Remarks and references to Appendices
RENINGHELST. (ALBERTA CAMP)	Sept 17.		The Battalion spent the day resting. 2nd Lts. G.R. BLACK – G.H. JOHNSON – A.W. RIDLEY – and R.R. KAY joined for duty. [initials]	
-do-	-18.		The Battalion attended a Smoke bomb demonstration in the morning & rested in the afternoon. Details left out of the line proceeded to CARNARVON CAMP at 5.0 pm. The Bn moved by route march to RIDGE WOOD via LA CLYTTE – HALLEBAST CORNER – BARDENBRUG leaving at 10 0 pm. Operation Order No 25 attached as Appendix V. [initials]	Appendix V
RIDGE WOOD	-19.		The Bn spent the day resting. At 8.0 pm the Bn (less details) moved up by route march to HEDGE ST. TUNNELS via ELSENWALLE – VOORMEZEELE – LOCK 8 – TOWSEY'S TRACK where it was accomodated in trenches. Operation Order No [illegible] attached as Appendix VI [initials]	Appendix VI
HEDGE ST.	-20		Attack Day. Zero hour 5.40 am. The 123rd Infty Bde were in support to the 122nd (on left) and 124th Inf Bdes which attacked at Zero, each on a front of two half Battalions. At 9.40 am orders were received for the Bn to move up to the original British Front Line between SHREWSBURY FOREST and BODMIN COPSE to dig in there. At 11.45 am on receipt of orders "D" Coy were sent to the right of the Division to assist the 124th Infty Bde to take the Blue Line (2nd Objectives) in front of which it had got held up by machine guns. At 11.55 am orders were received to move up to the Red Line (1st Objective) to dig in there	9.40 [initials]

(A7092). Wt. W12839/M1293. 750,000. 1/17. D. D. & L., Ltd. Forms/C.2118/14.

Instructions regarding War Diaries and Intelligence Summaries are contained in F. S. Regs., Part II. and the Staff Manual respectively. Title pages will be prepared in manuscript.

WAR DIARY
or
INTELLIGENCE SUMMARY.
(Erase heading not required.)

Army Form C. 2118.

20th Durham Light Infantry
for September 1917

Place	Date 1917	Hour	Summary of Events and Information	Remarks and references to Appendices
	Sept. 20	(Contd)	and to be ready to assist in the attack. On arrival there about 2.0 pm. orders were received to push on to the Blue Line to join up between the 122nd and 124th Infty Bdes as the latter had got held up in front of the BASSEVILLEBEEK. This was done and the Bn (less D. Coy) arrived in position about 3.0 pm. At 5.15 pm orders were received for the Bn (less D Coy.) to attack the Green Line (3rd objective on the forward slope of TOWER HAMLETS ridge) but this was not done owing to the orders being received too late. The Bn. then dug in on the backward slope of TOWER HAMLETS ridge over the BASSEVILLEBEEK. About 6 pm 'D' Coy returned and dug in. At this time the situation was very uncertain and apparently the right flank of the Bn. was "in the air" owing to the 124th Inf Bde having not crossed the beek. Throughout the day till evening the enemy kept shelling the ridge near SHREWSBURY FOREST and BODMIN COPSE. Casualties:- 2nd Lt. A.T. CHARLTON killed - 2nd Lts J. CORBET - C.S. CUNNINGHAM - A.H. GARDNER - A.G. RODEN wounded. 1 OR killed and 6 OR wounded. 2nd Lt E. RUSSELL evacuated sick. Captain J.T. SAUNDERS joined the Details for duty	
Near TOWER HAMLETS.	21st		At 7.0 am orders were received for the Bn. to attack the Green Line in conjunction with the 10th Bn Rl W Kent Regt which was on our left. At 9.8 am the Bn. went over	

(A7092). Wt. W12839/M1293. 750,000. 1/17. D. D. & L., Ltd. Forms/C.2118/14.

Instructions regarding War Diaries and Intelligence Summaries are contained in F. S. Regs., Part II. and the Staff Manual respectively. Title pages will be prepared in manuscript.

WAR DIARY
or
INTELLIGENCE SUMMARY.
(Erase heading not required.)

Army Form C. 2118.

20th Durham Light Infantry
for September 1917.

Place	Date 1917	Hour	Summary of Events and Information	Remarks and references to Appendices
Sept	21st	(Contd)	to attack on two half Company fronts. The barrage which was suppose to come down at 9.0 am. consisted of a few shells sent over at intervals and was in consequence insufficient to keep down the Enemy machine guns. The attack pushed out for about 200 yards when it was held up by machine guns and forced to dig in, but not before we had suffered heavy casualties. During the attack the Enemy sent over practically no shells and fired nothing but machine guns & rifles. About 3 pm the Enemy advance over TOWER HAMLETS ridge to counter attack but was driven back by our rifle fire and Lewis guns which inflicted heavy casualties. This counter attack was attempted without any barrage. About 4 pm the Enemy barraged the forward slope of the ridge in rear of the BASSEVILLE-BEEK and later put up a box barrage on our position. Under cover of this barrage he again (at about 7.40 pm) assembled for a counter attack but was driven off by our artillery (also Lewis gun & rifle fire). Casualties. Captain A. Humphrey D.S.O. – 2nd Lt. H. W. H. Cartwright and 33 O.R. killed – Lieut. Colonel G. McNICOLL D.S.O. (attached 26th Royal Fusiliers) Died of wounds – Capt E. SMITH. M.C., Capt H. SOUTHWELL, Lieut P. L. DOBINSON, 2nd Lieut W. S. PRUDHOE, 2nd Lt E. P. SMITH, 2nd Lt W. BAMBOROUGH (died of wounds 25.9.17) and 188 O.R. wounded.	

20th Durham Light Infantry

Army Form C. 2118.

for September 1917

Instructions regarding War Diaries and Intelligence Summaries are contained in F. S. Regs., Part II. and the Staff Manual respectively. Title pages will be prepared in manuscript.

WAR DIARY
or
INTELLIGENCE SUMMARY.
(Erase heading not required.)

Place	Date 1917	Hour	Summary of Events and Information	Remarks and references to Appendices
Near TOWER HAMLETS.	Sept 22nd		Enemy fairly quiet after counter attack of last night, though intermittent shelling of both sides continued during day. During the afternoon the enemy put up a barrage west of the BASSEVILLEBEEK but no action followed. Casualties killed 6 OR wounded ~~7~~ ~~8~~ 14 O.R. Missing 21 O.R. [initials]	
~~-do-~~	~~23rd~~			
-do-	- 23rd	1.0 am	The Battalion was relieved by the 13th Bn Royal Sussex Regt and marched back to MICMAC CAMP arriving there by 8.0 am. Casualties 2/Lt W.P. McGIBBON & 6 OR killed. 10. OR missing. [initials]	
MICMAC CAMP	- 23rd	8.0 am	The Battalion rested till 2.0 pm when it marched to HUBERTSHOEK Siding where it entrained ~~at~~ for CAESTRE. On arrival at CAESTRE the Bn detrained and marched to ST SYLVESTRE-CAPPEL where it was billeted. [initials]	
ST SYLVESTRE CAPPEL.	- 24th		The day was spent in inspections, cleaning up &c [initials]	
-do-	- 25th		The Bn paraded at 11.30 am for inspection by the Divisional Commander who presented medal ribbons to officers & men who received awards for gallantry at KLEIN ZILLEBEEK on 31st July. The following officers received decorations:- Captain H.F. WILSON M.C. RAMC. Lieut J.G.R. PACY M.C. Lieut L.W. SHEPHERDSON MC. The transport proceeded by route march to WORMHOUDT where it stayed the night before proceeding to TETEGHEM the next day [initials] A draft of 77 OR joined the Bn from the Base [initials]	

(A7092). Wt. W12839/M1293. 750,000. 1/17. D. D. & L., Ltd. Forms/C.2118/14.

Army Form C. 2118.

20th Durham Light Infantry

for September 1917

Instructions regarding War Diaries and Intelligence Summaries are contained in F. S. Regs., Part II. and the Staff Manual respectively. Title pages will be prepared in manuscript.

WAR DIARY
or
INTELLIGENCE SUMMARY.
(*Erase heading not required.*)

Place	Date 1917	Hour	Summary of Events and Information	Remarks and references to Appendices
St SYLVESTRE CAPPEL.	Sept. 26		The Battalion proceeded by buses from the Second Army to the Fourth Army at TETEGHEM. arriving there about 1.0pm. The transport joined the Bn. again from WORMHOUDT about 4 pm. The Bn was accomodated in billets for the night. G.A.S. Lt. O.O. No 78 attached as appendix	App VII
TETEGHEM.	-27.		The Bn proceeded by march route to ZUYDCOOTE leaving at 7.20 am. On arrival it took over from the 2/5th Bn Lanc. Fus: the SANITORIUM SECTION of the ZUYDCOOTE SUB SECTOR. The remainder of the day was observed as a rest. G.A.S. Lt. O.O. No 79 attached as appendix	App VIII
ZUYDCOOTE	-28		The day was spent in training under Company arrangements. The Bn bathed in the sea in the afternoon. G.A.S. Lt.	
-do-	-29.		Training under Coy arrangements. Bathing in the sea in afternoon. G.A.S. Lt.	
-do-	-30.		Church Parade on beach in morning. Bathing in the sea in afternoon. The remainder of the day was observed as a holiday. G.A.S. Lt.	

In the Field
1st October 1917.

R.C. Smith Lieut-Colonel,
Commanding 20th Bn Durham Light Infantry.

(A7092). Wt. W12839/M1293. 750,000. 1/17. D. D. & L., Ltd. Forms/C.2118/14.

OPERATION ORDER NO. 1. COPY NO. 1.

Ref. Map 27s S.E.

---

1. - **OBJECTIVE.** The Brigade will attack and take the three objectives - as shewn on the attached map - called the Red, Blue and Green Lines respectively.

General Line of Attack - 146 T.B.

The attack will take place on Tuesday, 4th inst.

Zero hour will be at 11.30 a.m.

The 20th Bn. Durham Light Infantry will be the centre Battalion.

On the Right...... 23rd Bn. Middlesex Regt.

On the Left....... 11th Bn. "Queen's" Regt.

In Brigade Reserve....... 10th Bn. R.W.Kent Regt.

2. - **FORMING UP.** The Battalion will form up on the tapes as shewn in the attacked sketch. There will be three tapes, one f r the front line of each of the attacking companies. These will be put out on the night of the 3/4th inst under the direction of 2/Lieut. E.P.Smith.

The right and left of each Company will be marked by boards with luminous paint on the night of the 2/3rd inst. O's.C. Coys. will arrange to send at least two guides per platoon to find the exact location of these boards.

The Forming-up Ground, as shewn on the attached map, is t be thoroughly reconnoitred both by day and night by all plato n and section commanders.

In forming up, platoons will be led to their respective positions by moving down the LEULINGHEM - SETQUES Road, and thence along the tapes to their respective companies.

2. - **METHOD OF ATTACK.** The enemy are holding modified lines f ~~xx~~ trenches but have placed machine guns in a series of shell holes and strong points.

At Zero plus 30 mins. the Battalion will be formed up on the tapes.

At Zero the artillery barrage will come down on approximately the enemy front line, where it will remain for 4 mins.

At Zero hour the Battalion will move forward until the fr nt line is as close as possible t o the barrage. At Zero plus 4 m ns. the barrage will lift off the front line and form a protectice barrage 100 yds. in rear, where it will stay for 30 mins.

As soon as it lifts off the front line, the leading company will rush into the area thus freed and kill or caprute every German found.

The second company will pass through the leading comoany as soon as they have mopped up , and form up for attack under the barrage.

At Zero plus 34 mins. the barrage will move forward by bounds of 100 yds. and will stop on a line 100 yds in rear of the second objective for 30 mins. During this pause, B Company will mop up the area freed and consolidate on the Blue Line.

Under this protective barrage, the third company will form up for attack on the third objective.

At Zero plus 100 mins. the barrage will lift off the Green Line to 100 yds. in rear of it, and at Zero plus 106 mins. will form a standing barrage 600 yds. in front of the final objective.

On reaching the final objective the third company will at nce light flares, re-organise andconsolidate,and will send forward 2 Lewis Gun Sections to form Strong Points, 200 yds. in front of the GREEN LINE.

On reaching the Red Line, A Company will fire Red Very Lights B Company will fire White Lights on reaching the Blue Line and C Company Green Lights on reaching the Green Line.

D Company will be held in Battalion Reserve and will act under the orders of the Commanding Officer.

4. - MEDICAL. The Medical Officer will establish his R. A.P. in the Sap in the old RESERV E LINE at W.16.c.5.6.

5. - COMMUNICATION. The Signalling officer will arrange for communication by runners between the four companies and Bn. H.Q. and between Bn. H.Q. and Brigade Forward Station at W.16.a.1.5.

6. - BATTALION H.Q. will be established in a deep dugout at W.22.b.2.8.

(SGD) W.C.BROWN. Capt. A/Adjt.
20th Bn. Durham Light Infantry.

3-9-1917.
Issued by runner at
Copies to:-
No. 1 War Diary.
No. 2 O.C. A Coy.
No. 3 O.C. B Coy.
No. 4 O.C. C Coy.
No. 5 O.C. D Coy.
No. 6 H.Q. 123rd Infantry Brigade.

Appendix II

SECRET   20TH BATTALION DURHAM LIGHT INFANTRY   COPY NO. 1.....

OPERATION ORDER NO. 22.

Ref. Map 36D N.E.......

1. The Battalion will proceed by March Route to the WALLON CAPPEL Area tomorrow, 14th inst.

The Battalion will rendezvous on the Road E.11.b.7.4. - E.11.b.6.9. with the head of the column at E.11.b.6.9. at 8.35 a.m. The Transport will be ready in the yard at E.11.b.7.9. at the same time to join the Battalion as it marches past.

Order of March - Buglers, H.Q., A, B, C, D, Transport.

2. Distances to be maintained - 100 yards between Battalions, 50 yards between Companies and 50 yards between rear of last Company and head of Transport.

3. HALTS. The column will halt at 10 minutes to each clock hour and start again at each clock hour.

There will be a long halt about 12.30 p.m. The exact time will be notified on the march.

4. Stretcher Bearers will parade in the rear of their Companies. Stretchers will be carried on the Maltese Cart.

5. ~~The mens' valises will be carried by lorries and will be stacked ready for loading by 6 a.m. at the following places:-~~

~~H.Q. & D Coy. - At Battalion H.Q.~~

~~B & C Coy. - At Church (E.11.a.8.7.)~~

~~A Coy & Transport - At Bridge E.11.b.6.9.~~

~~O's.C. Coys. will ensure that each man's kit is properly marked.~~

Officers' Valises and Mess Kits will be stacked at Battalion Headquarters by 7 a.m.

6. O's.C. Companies will render certificates that all billets occupied by their Companies are left clean on departure and that all money owing to inhabitants by officers has been paid.

7. Acknowledge.

G. A. Samuel
Lieut. for Adjutant,
20th Bn. Durham Light Infantry.

13th September 1917.

Issued by Runner at 6.45 p.m.

Copies to:-

No. 1 War Diary.
No. 2 O.C. A Coy.
No. 3 O.C. B Coy.
No. 4 O.C. C Coy.
No. 5 O.C. D Coy.
No. 6 Quartermaster.
No. 7 Transport Officer.
No. 8 Medical Officer.
No. 9 Signalling Officer.
No. 10 R.S.M.

[illegible] L.I. [illegible] Bn

OPERATION ORDER No 23.

[illegible] SHEET 27.

1/ The Bn will continue the march to [illegible] PINKBOOM head of the column to pass the Starting Point U 5 d 24 at 12.51 pm.

Order of March – Buglers, HQ, C. D. B. A Coy Transport.

Dress – Marching order steel helmets will be carried.

2/ The following distances will be maintained on the march:–

380 yds	between	Battalions.
100 "	"	20th D.L.I. & T.M.B.
50 "	"	each unit & its Transport
50 "	"	Companies.

3/ **HALTS** There will be a long halt of $1\frac{1}{2}$ hours when the head of the column reaches CHESTRE (about 2.15 pm). The exact time of this halt will be notified on the march.

Apart from the long halt, normal halts will be observed.

4/ Officers' valises & Mess Kits will be stacked by 11.0 am at Coy H.Qrs, and the G.S. Wagon will call for these.

5/ O.C. Coys. will render to this office certificates mentioned in Para [illegible] of O.O. No 22 d/15-9-17.

6. Reveille – 6 a.m. Breakfast [illegible]
Sick Parade (urgent cases only) – 9.30 a.m.

[signature]
Lt A/Adjutant
20th Bn Durham L. I.

14-9-17
Issued by runner at

Copies to
No 1 War Diary
No 2 O/c A Coy
No 3 " B "
No 4 " C "
No 5 " D
No 6 M.O.
No 7 Q.M. & T.O.
No 8 R.S.M.
No 9 [illegible]
No 10 F.L.O.

[illegible]

[illegible]

1. [illegible] Battalion will continue the march to ALBERTA CAMP RENINGHELST tomorrow [illegible] to leave the Starting Point the X rds at 45 [illegible] (K.4.c.3.4) at 10.16 a.m.

Order of march [illegible] D C A B transport.

HQrs + [illegible] Bn.

Coys will leave the Starting Point at the following times:-

H.Q. - 10.16 a.m.   A Coy 10.19 a.m.

D Coy - 10.17 a.m.   B Coy 10.20 a.m.

C Coy - 11.18 a.m.

O.C. Coys are to ensure that Coys leave their [illegible] exactly to time.

The Second Officer will arrange watches to be synchronised at 8 a.m.

2. [illegible] (to be [illegible])

3. Officers [illegible] will be [illegible] in [illegible] by 9 a.m. and the [illegible] 11 a.m. [illegible] for them.

The packs of C & D Coys will be stacked at the Road Junction at X.[illegible] by 8 a.m. where a lorry will call for them.

The packs of A & B Coys and [illegible]

2.

will be [illegible] the [illegible] [illegible].
[illegible] [illegible] [illegible] lorry and
[illegible] [illegible].
[illegible] [illegible] will [illegible] detail [illegible] [illegible]
[illegible] proceed [illegible] [illegible] [illegible] by lorry.
[illegible] [illegible] [illegible] [illegible] in the second
lorry. [illegible] will be [illegible]
[illegible] [illegible] [illegible] the [illegible] [illegible] by
[illegible].

4. [illegible] [illegible] [illegible] [illegible] (14.4.17) [illegible]
[illegible] [illegible] [illegible] tomorrow.

5. [illegible] [illegible] [illegible] [illegible] [illegible]
arrangements.
[illegible] [illegible] [illegible] [illegible] [illegible]

1. [illegible] [illegible]

[illegible] [illegible] [illegible] [illegible] [illegible]
[illegible] [illegible] [illegible]

[illegible] 1 [illegible]
2 [illegible]
3
4
5
6 [illegible]
7 [illegible]
8 [illegible]
9 [illegible] [illegible]
10 [illegible] [illegible]

APPENDIX V

20TH BN. DURHAM LIGHT INFANTRY. COPY NO. 1

OPERATION ORDER NO. 28.

Ref.Map - 28 S.W.

---

1. The Battalion will continue the march to the RIDGE WOOD AREA today,18th Sept., in accordance with the attached March Table.

2. Orders for the Transport will be issued later.

3. Normal Halts will be observed.

4. Dress - Fighting Order with great-coats.

5. O's C Coys. will render the certificate re billets to this office by 6.0 p.m.

5. Officer's Kits and Mess Kits will be stacked at the GUARD Room by 5.30 p.m. The Transport Officer will arrange for the necessary Transport. Orders as to men's packs have been issued.

6. All Units moving before 7.45 p.m. will maintain ¼mile between platoons.

7. The Signal Officer will arrange for watches to be synchronised at 5.0 p.m.

8. ACKNOWLEDGE.

18-9-17. Lieut. A/Adjutant.

Issued by runner at

Copies to:-

No. 1 War Diary.
No. 2 O.C. A Coy.
No. 3 O.C. B Coy.
No. 4 O.C. C Coy.
No. 5 O.C. D Coy.
No. 6 Q.M. & T.O.
No. 7 Medical Officer.
No. 8 Signall Officer.
No. 9 R.S.M.
No. 10 Filed.

TIME TABLE.

Serial No	Unit	From	To	Route	Starting Point.	Time for head to pass S.P.	Time for head to pass M.6.a.9.7
4a	A Coy.	WESTOUTRE Area No 6	RIDGE WOOD AREA	via Junction Road & Track M.6 a.9.7. -LA CLYTTE HALLEBAST CORNER	Junction of Road & Track M.5.a 25.10	6.22 p.m.	6.40 p.m.
4b	B Coy.	-do-	-do-	-do-	-do-	6.42 p.m	7.0p.m.
4c	H.Q.	-do-	-do-	-do-	-do-	7.2 p.m.	7.20 p.m.
5a	C Coy.	-do-	-do-	-do-	-do-	7.57 p.m.	8.15 p.m.
5b	D Coy.	-do-	-do-	-do-	-do-	8.2 p.m.	8.20 p.m.

Note.-

4a. - Distance of ½ mile to be kept between platoons.
4b. - -do- -do- -do-
4c. - Will march as one-platoon ½ mile in rear of B Coy.
5a. - 50 yards distance between platoons.
5b. - -do- -do-

181

APPENDIX VI

SECRET

20TH BN. DURHAM LIGHT INFANTRY. COPY NO. 1

OPERATION ORDER NO. 26.

Ref. Map 28 & Map 'B'

1. The Battalion will march to its assembly area in ARMAGH WOOD on a date to be notified later.
Order of March - H.Q., A, B, C & D Coys.
Head of the Column to be at N 5 b 4.8. at 8.0 a.m.
A distance of 50 yards will be maintained between platoons.
Normal Halts will be observed.
H.Q. will drop two men at every X Roads or point where the route is at all complicated. These men will wait and see the whole Battalion follows the correct route and then fall in with the last platoon.
Route - TRACK north of VOORMEZEELE thence TOWSEY'S WALK.

2. Completion of xxxxxx assembly will be reported to H.Q. by runner.

3. Instructions re Officers' Kits and Men's Great-coats will be issued later.

4. The usual certificate re billets will be forwarded to the Adjutant by 7.30 p.m.

Lieut.
A/Adjutant.

19-9-17.
Issued by runner at 2.0 p.m.
Copies to :-
No. 1 War Diary.
No. 2. O.C. A Coy.
No. 3. O.C. B Coy.
No. 4 O.C. C Coy.
No. 5 O.C. D Coy
No 6 M.O.
No 7 Q.M. & T.O.
No. 8 R.S.M.
No. 9 Sig. Officer.
No. 10 Filed.

APPENDIX VII

SECRET

20TH BN. DURHAM LIGHT INFANTRY   COPY NO. 1
OPERATION ORDER NO. 28

---

1. The Battalion will parade on the road near the Quartermaster's Stores facing North, in column of route, in the order Headquarters, A,B,C,D Coy, with the head of the column at the railway crossing F 34 a 3.2., ready to move off at 5.50 a.m. tomorrow, 26th inst.
Dress -- Marching Order.

2. They will proceed by bus to the TETEGHEM AREA, leaving at 7.0 a.m. from the ST.SYLVESTER CAPPEL - HAZEBROUCK ROAD.
The numbers of the busses allotted to the battalion are 159 to 188. Each bus must carry 22 men. Vehicles will be marked in chalk. Numbers painted on vehicles should be ignored.

3. An extra vehicle will be placed between No's 52 & 53 for a party of 5 Officers (One to be detailed by each O.C.Coy. & one from H.Q. who will proceed to BRAYDUNES. These officers will report to a representative of the 123rd Inf.Bde. at H.Q. 197 th Inf.Bde. for the purpose of taking over details of Coast-Defence Sub-Sector. These officers will be ready to embuss at the embussing point at 6.45 a.m.

4. Officer's valises and Mess Kits, and all dixies will be stacked at the Q.M.Stores by 5.30 a.m. A lorry will call for these.

Lieut.
A/Adjutant.

25-9-17.
Issued by runner at 11.10 p.m.
Copies to:-
No 1 War Diary.
No.2 O.C. A Coy.
No.3 O.C. B Coy.
No.4 O.C. C Coy.
No.5 O.C. D Coy.
No.6 Medical officer.
No.7 R.S.M.
No.8 R.Q.M.S.
No.9 Lieut L.W.Shepherdson
No.10 Filed.

APPENDIX VIII

SECRET. 20th Bn. DURHAM L.I. OPERATION ORDER NO. 29. Copy No..../

1. The Battalion will relieve the 2/7th Bn. Lanc. Fus. in the centre section of ZUYDCOOTE Coast Defence, tomorrow 27th inst.
2. The Battalion will parade at the Road Junction near Bn.H.Q. ready to move off at 7.20 a.m. Dress - Full Marching Order. Order of March - H.Q., A,B,C,D, Transport.
3. 200 yards distance will be maintained between Coys. and between Coys. and Transport. Normal halts will be observed.
4. Officers' Valises and Mess Kits of H.Q., B,C,D Coy will be stacked at their Billets by 6.15 a.m. O.C. A Coy. will arrange for valises and mess kits of his Coy. tobe stacked at the Q.M.Stores by 6.30 a.m.
5. Each Company will have a sentry group of 1 N.C.O. & 3 men detailed before marching off to take over from a sebtry group of the opposite number. O.C. 2/7th Lanc. Fus. has arranged for guides to be at the Bridge near the Centre Section to guide these groups to their posts. Posts will be numbered as under.- A Coy. - No.8. B Coy - No. 5. D Coy. - No. 6. C Coy. - No. 7.
N.C.O's i/c Posts will get all information from the relieved N.C.O's.
6. Guides will meet each platoon and H.Q. at the Bxridge to guide them to their Billet.
7. The usual certificate re Billets will be rendered to O.Room by 7 am.
8. Acknowledge.

(SGD) C.A.BAMLET. Lt.A/Adjt.

26-9-1917.
Issued by runnr at 8 p.m.
Copies to:-

No. 1 Filed.	No. 6. Quartermaster.
No. 2 O.C. A Coy.	No. 7 T.O.
No. 3 O.C. B Coy.	No. 8 M.O.
No. 4 O.C. C Coy.	No. 9 2nd in Command.
No. 5 O.C. D Coy.	No. 10.R,S.M.

20th Bn. Durham L.I.

DAILY STATE

	OFFS	OR'S	TOTAL
Present with Coys	24	751	778
do HQ	6	81	87
Transport Section	1	47	48
Q.M Estab	1	16	17
2nd Army	1	2	3
Xth Corps HQ	–	–	–
Divl Employ	2	4	6
Bde do	–	7	7
Attd to A.S.C	–	1	1
do M.G.C	–	24	24
Courses	2	34	36
In FA & D.R.S	3	23	26
On Leave	–	4	4
Pigeon Personnel	–	3	3
attd 233 Field Coy RE	1	35	36
228 do	–	1	1
Rest Camp	1	7	8
26th Bn Royal Fusiliers	–	1	1
D.A.D.O.S	–	1	1
Trade Test	–	1	1
Absentees	–	2	2
	39	1020	1059
	39	10	

1-9-17.

20th Durham L.I.

DAILY STATE.

Present with Coys	23	705	728
do HQ	4	79	83
Transport Section	1	46	47
Q.M. Estab.	1	17	18
2nd Army	1	2	3
X" Corps	—	1	1
Divl Employ	–	2	2
Bde do	–	10	10
Attd to A.S.C	–	1	1
Coy M.G.C	-	23	23
Courses of Instr.	4	35	39
In FA & D.R.S.	1	7	8
Pigeon Personnel	—	3	3
On Leave	1	4	5
233 Field Coy R.E.	1	36	37
228 do	—	1	1
Up the Line	1	10	11
D.A.D.O.S	–	1	1
Trade Test	–	1	1
Rest Camp	-	10	10
Course in England	1	1	2
absentee	–	2	2
17th Bn Royal Fusiliers	1	1	2
On Escort Duty	-	2	2
TOTAL	40	1000	1040

15-9-17.

CONGRATULATORY MESSAGE.

The Divisional Commander congratulates all ranks on the splendid spirit with which the attack was made, and the determined way in which many strong points and difficult points were dealt with. The result of the two days fighting calls for high praise for all concerned. It has given the enemy another experience of the fighting qualities of the 41st Division.

22nd September 1917. (SD) R. PARKER. Lt.Colonel, G.S.

20th Bn Durham L I
DAILY STATE

	Off's	OR's	Total
Present with Coy	14	495	508
do HQ	5	66	71
Transport Section	1	49	50
Q.M Estab	1	17	18
2nd Army	1	2	3
Xth Corps	–	1	1
Divl Employ	–	2	2
Bde -do-	–	24	24
Attd to A.S.C	–	1	1
123 M.G.C	–	23	23
238 do	–	22	22
Courses	1	22	23
Hospital	2	23	25
Pigeon Personnel	–	3	3
Leave	1	12	13
233 Field Coy	1	34	35
228 do	–	1	1
19th Ordnance Mobile Workshops	–	1	1
D.A.D.O.S	–	1	1
Trade Test	–	1	1
Attd 26th Bn R F's	–	1	1
Absentee	–	1	1
Area Commandants Office BERTHEN	–	1	1
Xth Corps Musk & Rein Camp	2	4	6
Course in England	1	–	1
Rest Camp	–	12	12
	30	819	849

29-9-17

CONGRATULATORY MESSAGE.

The Divisional Commander desires me to convey to the Brigade his congratulations on the determined manner in which they attempted to complete the capture of the GREEN LINE. The fighting spirit shown, and the bold effort made by them, deserve the highest praise. The Battalions well maintained and added to their previous good reputation, and the Divisional Commander thanks them sincerely for their splendid efforts.

(SGD) E. P. SEROCOLD.
Brigadier-General,
Commanding 123rd Infantry Brigade.

20th Bn Durham L.I.

DAILY STATE

	OFF'S	ORS	TOT.
Present with Coys	24	726	750
do HQ	5	88	93
Transport Section	1	47	48
Q.M. Estab.	1	16	17
Second Army	1	2	3
X" Corps HQ	–	–	–
Divl Employ	–	2	2
Bde do	–	5	5
Attd to A.S.C.	–	1	1
do M.G.C	–	24	24
Courses	3	34	37
In F A & D R S.	1	18	19
Pigeon Personnel	–	3	3
On Leave	1	6	7
Attd 233 Field Coy R E	1	36	37
228 do	–	1	1
D A D O S	–	1	1
Attd 26" Bn Royal Fusiliers	1	1	2
Trade Test	–	1	1
Rest Camp	–	6	6
Course in England	1	1	2
Absentees	–	2	2
TOTAL	40	1021	1061

8-9-17

130

Instructions regarding War Diaries and Intelligence Summaries are contained in F. S. Regs., Part II. and the Staff Manual respectively. Title pages will be prepared in manuscript.

WAR DIARY
or
~~INTELLIGENCE SUMMARY.~~

(Erase heading not required.) 20th Battn Durham Light Infantry

Vol 18

Army Form C. 2118.

Place	Date	Hour	Summary of Events and Information	Remarks and references to Appendices
ZUYDCOTE	Oct 1st		The Battalion paraded under the Commanding Officer for Battalion Drill on the sands, after which training was carried out under Coy arrangements. Sea Bathing by Coys after 3.30 p.m. S	
	" 2nd		Battalion Drill, Coy training and Sea Bathing exactly as above. The G.O.C lectured all officers at 5.30 p.m. S	
	" 3rd		Parades as on October 1st & 2nd. S	
	" 4th		Weather very wet Coys confined to Billets for training. S	
	5th		The Battalion moved from ZUYDCOTE to ST IDESBALDE preparatory to taking over the left sector of the Divisional front, from the 1/7th Manchester Regt. S	
ST IDESBALDE	6TH		At 5.45 p.m the Battalion moved up to the trenches and relieved the 1/7th MANCHESTER REGT. A fair amount of shelling was experienced on the way up and 4 O.R.s were wounded. S	
Trenches	7th		Weather during day very wild & wet. During the Night a patrol of 1 offr & 3 men patrolled along the shore & were fired at with minenwerfers but returned safe. About 10 pm we were shelled pretty heavily in the vicinity of B Coy H.Qrs, and had 4 casualties Wounded ~~killed and wounded~~ ~~through the Shell Shock at 10 H.S.~~ NWT.	

(A 6092). Wt. W12839/M1293. 750,000. 1/17. D. D. & L., Ltd. Forms/C.2118/14.

Army Form C. 2118.

Instructions regarding War Diaries and Intelligence Summaries are contained in F. S. Regs., Part II. and the Staff Manual respectively. Title pages will be prepared in manuscript.

WAR DIARY
or
~~INTELLIGENCE SUMMARY.~~
(*Erase heading not required.*) 20 Batt Durham Light Infantry.

Place	Date	Hour	Summary of Events and Information	Remarks and references to Appendices
Trenches.	8th		Weather very wild & wet. During the night a patrol of 6 O.R. went out and reported Flashes from Pocket Torch in the Enemies lines. They returned safe. During the day we were shelled pretty heavily. We had no Casualties. Lieut Eppstein rejoins Batt from Base. Transferred from 1/6 Manchesters. NWT	
Trenches	9th		Weather very wild & wet. A patrol of 4 O.R went out at 9.30 pm & returned at 11.30 pm, seeing no sign of Enemy. We were shelled heavily during the day with 5.9's 4.2 hows & Minnies but had no casualties. Capt Crawford rejoins Batt from Divisional Wing & is attached to "B" Coy. NWT	
Trenches	10th		Weather very windy with occasional rain showers. The patrol of 4 O.R went out as usual, and reported nothing of importance. The shelling was not so heavy as usual, owing to the Activity of our Airmen. We had a few shots over our lines from Snipers, which was unusual, but had no casualties. NWT	
Trenches	11th		Weather fine but windy. The day was unusually quiet & very little shelling. We were relieved at night by the 23 Batt Middlesex. The relief being complete at midnight. We then proceeded to Middlesex Camp. "A" Coy were not relieved, and six of our Lewis Gun teams took over the Aerial Defences from the Middlesex. NWT	
Middlesex Camp	12.		Weather fine in Morning but very wet in the Afternoon. The Companies were inspected by the M.O. and Kit & Rifle inspections were held under Coy Arrangements. 2Lt Brown rejoins from Leave. NWT	
	13.		Weather Showery. Parades at 9. am under Company Arrangements in Musketry & Gas. The Pay Parades were arranged in the Afternoon. Lieut Pacy rejoins from leave. NWT	

(A7092). Wt. W12839/M1293. 750,000. 1/17. D. D. & L., Ltd. Forms/C.2118/14.

Instructions regarding War Diaries and Intelligence Summaries are contained in F. S. Regs., Part II. and the Staff Manual respectively. Title pages will be prepared in manuscript.

WAR DIARY
or
INTELLIGENCE SUMMARY.
(Erase heading not required.)

Army Form C. 2118.

20th Batt Durham L. I.

Place	Date	Hour	Summary of Events and Information	Remarks and references to Appendices
MIDDLESEX CAMP.	14.		Weather fine. Voluntary Services were carried out in the YMCA. hut by the Chaplain Rev. Dunn. R.C.s Services were held in OOST. DUNKIRKE BAINS Church.	MWS
do	15.		Weather fine. We were relieved by the K.R.R.s at 1pm, and proceeded to "A" Camp BRAY. DUNES. MWT	
BRAY DUNES	16.		The Battalion paraded under Coy. arrangements, for Musketry Skirmishing. PT & BF	
"	17		The Battalion paraded under Coy arrangements, for do do	MW
"	18.		The morning parades same as previous day. In the afternoon Outposts were practised under Coy Arrangements. Capt Crawford assumed command of 'A' Coy. The Commanding Officer went on leave MWT.	
"	19.		~~2 Lieut T S DUDDY reported for duty & is posted to 'A' Coy~~. The remaining Coys ABCD carried out training for Open Warfare & Outposts. At 3.30pm there was an Officers riding class. 'C' Coy paraded for Boat Building & Crossing the Canal.	
	20th		The Commanding Officer inspected A Coy in full Marching Order. The remaining coys carried out training in Open Warfare, and in the afternoon, an inter-platoon football Competition was carried out by Coys	
	21st		The Batt paraded and marched to the West Kents parade ground for service by the Rev. C S Dunn.	
	22nd		The Battalion marched to ADINKIRQUE, where they practised crossing the canal on rafts. Coys training was carried out for an hour in the afternoon. AB 2/Lt	2/Lt H. WATERS reported for duty with the Batt AB 2/Lt

(A7092). Wt. W12839/M1293. 750,000. 1/17. D. D. & L., Ltd. Forms/C.2118/14.

Instructions regarding War Diaries and Intelligence Summaries are contained in F. S. Regs., Part II. and the Staff Manual respectively. Title pages will be prepared in manuscript.

WAR DIARY
or
~~INTELLIGENCE SUMMARY.~~
(Erase heading not required.)

Army Form C. 2118.

20th Battn Durham L I

Place	Date	Hour	Summary of Events and Information	Remarks and references to Appendices
BRAY DUNES	Oct 23rd		The Battalion marched to ADINKIRQUE in order to practise crossing the canal on rafts but owing to the wet weather the Battalion marched back without carrying out the practice. AB	
"	24"		Coy training was carried out, attacks on Strong Points box respirators drill, etc. D coy were at B range. 2/Lt AD PARSONS reported for duty AB	
	25"		The Battalion relieved the 16th Lanc Fus in the BRAY DUNES sector of the ZUDCOOTE coast defence sub-sector. Relief was completed by 10. AM. 2/Lieut G LISTER reported for duty, & posted to C coy. AB	
	26"		8.30 AM to 12.30 p.m. Coy training was carried out by A & D coys, 1 hours drill & movement in box respirators. C coy practised ~~At 4.15 p.m.~~ crossing canal. B were on the range.	
	~~27"~~		At 4.15 p.m. HQrs "A B & D" coys marched to ADINKIRQUE to practice crossing the canal, but marched back without having carried out the practice owing to the R.E. coy not turning up. 2/Lieuts PL DAVIES, WJ SCOTT, & A GRAHAM reported for duty. AB	
	27"		Coy training was carried out from 8.30 AM to 12.30 p.m., & from 2 p.m to 3.30 p.m. D coy were on the range. AB	

(A7092). Wt. W12839/M1293. 750,000. 1/17. D. D. & L., Ltd. Forms/C.2118/14.

Instructions regarding War Diaries and Intelligence Summaries are contained in F. S. Regs., Part II. and the Staff Manual respectively. Title pages will be prepared in manuscript.

WAR DIARY
or
~~INTELLIGENCE SUMMARY.~~

(*Erase heading not required.*)

Army Form C. 2118.

28th Bn Durham L.I.

Place	Date Oct 1917	Hour	Summary of Events and Information	Remarks and references to Appendices
BRAY DUNES	28th		R.C. church parade in BRAY DUNES church at 9 A.M. The rest of the day was devoted to sports. 2/Lieut V CARMICHEAL reported for duty. AB	
"	29th		Owing to the Battalion having been ordered to prepare to move the day was spent in kit inspections, & refitting the Battalion. 2/Lieut W.A DAVIDSON reported for duty. AB	
"	30th		A B & D coys spent the day in sand-bagging the huts in the camp. C coy carried out coy training, firing Lewis Guns out to sea, & practiced firing rifle grenades. AB	
"	31st		All officers & N.C.Os took tactical exercises under Major S.M. The subject was advance guards. The Battalion went for a route march. Coy training from 2 to 4.30 p.m was carried out, subjects fire control & outposts. AB	

R C Smith Lt Col.
Cmdg 28th D.L.I.

(A7092). Wt. W12839/M1293. 750,000. 1/17. D. D. & L., Ltd. Forms/C.2118/14.

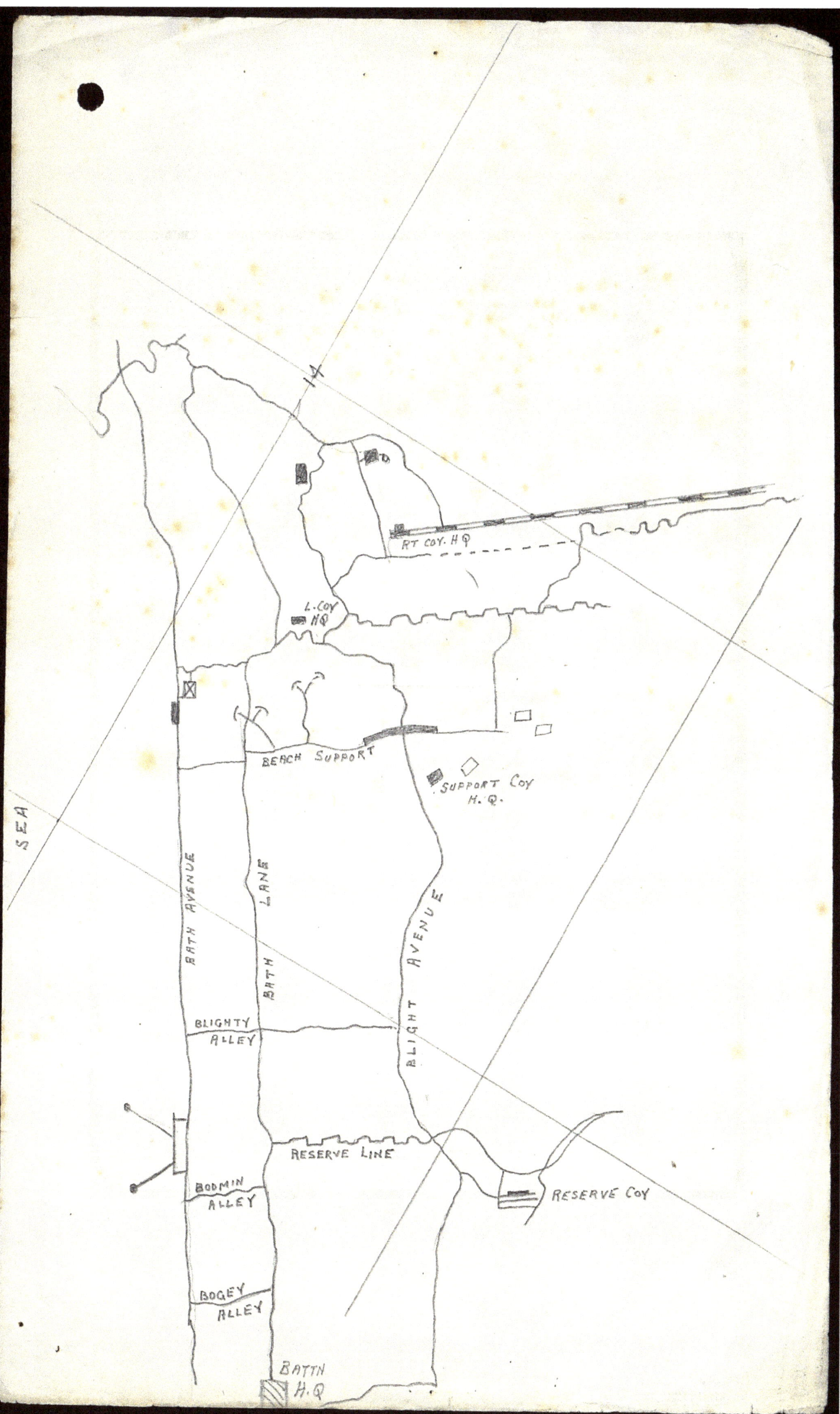

RT COY. H.Q
L. COY H.Q
BEACH SUPPORT
SUPPORT COY H.Q.
SEA
BATH AVENUE
BATH LANE
BLIGHT AVENUE
BLIGHTY ALLEY
RESERVE LINE
RESERVE COY
BODMIN ALLEY
BOGEY ALLEY
BATTN H.Q

20th BN. DURHAM. L. I. 27-10-17

DAILY STATE.

	OFF	OR's	TOT
Present with Coys.	19	508	527
-do- HQ	5	84	89
Transport Section	1	53	54
Q.M. Establishment	1	17	18
Army HQ	–	1	1
Divisional Employ	1	3	4
Brigade -do-	–	8	8
A.S.C.	–	1	1
Brigade Class	–	5	5
Courses of Instruction	4	43	47
In F.A. + D.R.S.	–	39	39
Pigeon Personnel	–	3	3
Hutting Work	–	13	13
On Leave	2	33	35
Attd 233 Field Coy R.E.	1	29	30
do 228 -do-	–	1	1
Area Commandants Office BERTHEN	–	1	1
Camp Commandant 41st Div.	–	1	1
Course in England	1	–	1
124 Bde Signals	–	1	1
Devl Wing Reinforcements	–	223	223
-do- Staff	1	10	11
Absentee	–	1	1
TOTAL	36	1081	1117

1. War Diary

Operation Orders No.75 by Capt. A. Mc.K.Reid, M.C.
Commanding 123rd Company, M. G. Corps.

Ref. map CONEGLIANO
1/50,000.

1. The 123rd Coy, M.G.C. will be relieved by the 68th Coy, M.G.C., in the left sub-sector on evening 24th/25th February, in accordance with attached table "A" and will move to CA.MIANE on February 25th in accordance with attached table "B".

2. All details of work in progress, particulars of night firing lines, alternative positions, accomodation and all trench stores and area stores will be handed over, and receipts for same sent to. C.H.Q.

3. All belt boxes, petrol cans, T bases, telephones and telescopes etc will be brought out by all gun teams.

4. On completion of relief wire "DEMOCRAT".

5. On march on 25th to CA.MIANE.
   Dress:- Full marching order with packs. Steel helmet slung on left shoulder, water bottles full.
   Limbers:- Packed as previously by 8.30 am.
   Blankets:- Rolled in bundles of 20 and dumped outside main billet by 8.30 am. Sgt. Mackie will be detailed as guide.

6. Limber with cooks' stores will start out immediately after breakfast and prepare meal at CA.MIANE. on arrival.

7. Acknowledge.

Dunklin Captain

24.2.18. Commanding 123rd Coy, M. G. Corps.

Table "A"

Date	Relieving Secs: 123.Coy	68.Coy	2 guides per Section at Place	Time	LIMBERS No.	Place	Time	On relief
24/25th	Sec.1		CORNER HOUSE	6.50pm	1 & 2	Sec.H.Q.	8pm.	Secs move independently to billets at BIADENE vacated by 124th Coy M.G.C.
"	2		"	"	(Limbers with Sectn)			
"	3		"	"	5 & 6	Sec.H.Q.	8.15p	
"	4		"	"	7 & 8	Sec.H.Q.	8.10p	
"	H.Q. (1 guide)		"	"	"B",H.Q, & messcart at H.Q.		7pm	

REMARKS All bulk ammunition and surplus gun stores will be placed in limbers before leaving Transport Lines so that limbers may remain at BIADENE on night 24th/25th.

Table. "B"

Date		From	To.	Parade
25th Feb.	Coy & Transport complete	BIADENE	CA.MIANE	For moving off, 9.30 am outside billet at BIADENE.

REMARKS Normal halts for 10 mins at 10 mins to each clock hour will be observed. No dinner halt.

171

From O.C. 11th (S) Bn The Queen's Regt

To D.A.G.'s Office
Base.

I beg to forward herewith War Diary for May, which I regret has not been forwarded before, owing to it being overlooked.

R C Smith Capt for Lt Col
Cmdg 11th Bn Queens Regt.

18-6-16

20th BN DURHAM. L. I   20-10-17

DAILY STATE

	OFF	OR'S	TOT
Present with Coys	13	519	532
do HQ	5	83	88
Transport Section	1	54	55
Q.M. Establishment	1	16	17
Army Headquarters	–	1	1
Divisional Employ	1	4	5
Brigade -do-	–	8	8
A.S.C	–	1	1
Courses of Instruction	4	35	39
In FA + DRS.	1	44	45
Pigeon Personnel	–	3	3
Netting Work	–	13	13
Attd 233 Field Coy. R.E.	1	28	29
" 228 -do-	–	1	1
Area Commandants Office BERTHEN	–	1	1
Trade Test	–	1	1
D.A.D.O.S	–	1	1
Course in England	1	–	1
124 Bde Signals	1	1	2
Divisional Wing (Reinforcements)	–	211	211
-do- Staff	1	8	9
Absentee	–	1	1
TOTAL	31	1075	1106

20th BN. DURHAM. L.I. 13-10-17

DAILY STATE

	OFF's	OR's	TOT
Present with Coys.	10	535	545
do HQ	6	86	92
Transport Section	1	48	49
Q. M. Establishment	–	16	16
Army Headquarters	–	1	1
Divisional Employ	–	3	3
Brigade - do -	–	8	8
A. S. C	–	1	1
Course of Instruction	~~4~~ 4	48	52
In F A & D. R. S	1	23	24
Pigeon Personnel	–	3	3
On Leave	3	38	41
Attd 233 Field Coy R E	1	30	31
228 - do -	–	1	1
Area Commandants Office BERTHEN	–	1	1
19th Ordnance Mobile Workshops	–	1	1
Trade Test	–	1	1
D. A. D. O. S	–	1	1
Course in England	1	–	1
Escort & Prisoner	–	3	3
Hospital with Officer	–	1	1
Divl Wing Reinforcements	–	195	195
- do - Staff	1	7	8
absentee	–	1	1
	29	1053	1082

20th BN. DURHAM. L. I 6-10-17

DAILY STATE

	OFF'S	OR'S	TOT.
Present with Coys	11	605	616
do H.Q.	5	81	86
Transport Section	1	48	49
Q.M. Establishment.	–	17	17
Army Headquarters	1	2	3
Divisional Employ	–	3	3
Brigade -do-	–	9	9
A.S.C	–	1	1
Courses of Instruction	3	27	30
In FA & DRS	–	26	26
Pigeon Personnel	–	3	3
On Leave	3	24	27
233 Field Coy R.E.	1	32	33
228 -do-	–	1	1
Ordnance Mobile Workshops	–	1	1
Area Commandant BERTHEN	–	1	1
D.A.D.O.S	–	1	1
Trade Test	–	1	1
1st Corps Musketry & Rein Camp	2	4	6
Divl Wing	–	173	173
Divl Guard	–	8	8
Course in England	1	–	1
TOTAL	28	1070	1098

www.ingramcontent.com/pod-product-compliance
Lightning Source LLC
Chambersburg PA
CBHW081352160426
43192CB00013B/2394

* 9 7 8 1 4 7 4 5 2 0 4 4 7 *